W9-BXZ-004

THE USBORNE INTRODUCTION TO
MODERN ART

The picture on the previous page is part of *A Bigger Splash*, by David Hockney. You can see the whole picture on pages 58-59.

These pages show an enlarged detail from *Dynamic Suprematism*, by Kasimir Malevich. The whole picture is reproduced on page 31.

THE USBORNE INTRODUCTION TO
MODERN ART

Rosie Dickins

Consultant:
Tim Marlow

Edited by Jane Chisholm
American Editor: Carrie Armstrong
Designed by Vici Leyhane and
Catherine-Anne MacKinnon

Picture research by Ruth King

Contents

👁 Internet links

Look for Internet link boxes throughout this book. They contain descriptions of websites where you can find out more about modern art. For links to these websites, go to the **Usborne Quicklinks Website** at **www.usborne-quicklinks.com** and type the keywords "modern art."

The websites described in this book are regularly reviewed and the links in **Usborne Quicklinks** are updated. However, the content of a website may change at any time and Usborne Publishing is not responsible for the content of any website other than its own. Please follow the Internet safety guidelines on page 87.

These pages show a detail from *Stables* (1913), by Franz Marc. You can see the whole picture on page 21.

What is modern art?

Modern art can be anything from an elaborate oil painting to a melting snowball or an empty room with the light going on and off. Surprisingly, people use the term "modern art" to describe art from as far back as the 1850s. That might not sound very modern, but it was about then that artists began to rethink their goals and ideas in a very radical way.

Spot the difference

For hundreds of years, most artists tried to create the illusion of real, 3-D scenes. But in the 19th century that began to change – partly because of the invention of photography in the 1830s. Before then, people had relied on artists to capture appearances. Once photographs could do that, some artists felt they should be doing something else. Also, in the past many artists had been paid by wealthy people to work for them. But that changed during the 19th century too. Artists began to create art first and sell it later, which gave them more freedom to experiment.

Just compare the two paintings on this page. Both show arrangements of objects, or still lifes – a traditional subject for painters. But the differences are far more obvious than the similarities.

Vanitas (1600s), by an unknown French artist; oil on canvas. *Vanitas* is Latin for "vanity" – meaning the vanity or emptiness of earthly pleasures when we all die in the end.

Guitar on a Table (1916), by Juan Grís; oil on canvas, 36 x 24in. Notice how Grís uses geometric shapes to break up the picture, and there are odd jumps between one shape and the next, so things don't join up.

Original works

Many people judge art by the technical skill of the artist – so they are more impressed by polished, lifelike paintings, such as the skull, than experimental art, such as the guitar. But for many artists nowadays, originality is more important than technique. The skull might look very convincing, but the simple shapes and vivid colors of the guitar make it a very striking, inventive image.

Is it really art?

Now there is such a huge emphasis on being original, it isn't surprising that artists are constantly pushing the boundaries of what we call "art." If you visit an art gallery today, you might see a completely white canvas, a bottle rack, a row of pebbles, a huge, hamburger-shaped cushion, or a pile of trash left from a party.

Does that sound like art to you? The word "art" originally meant "made by people," but some of these things weren't even made by the artist. They were just things he or she had found. You might not expect to come across them in a gallery at all. Does seeing them there make them art?

The Physical Impossibility of Death in the Mind of Someone Living (1991), by Damien Hirst; tiger shark, 5% formaldehyde, glass, steel, 84 x 204 x 84in. This is a real, dead shark, suspended in formaldehyde to stop it from decaying.

The shock of the new

A lot of modern art sets out to be new and shocking, in order to startle you and make you see things in a new way. But, when you look at it closely, modern art often turns out to be about age-old themes. Damien Hirst became notorious for using dead animals, such as the shark above. But he uses it to explore mortality, just like the 17th-century oil painting on the left. The shark's preserved body, like the painted skull, is meant to make us think about death. But it looks so alive, it is hard to accept it is really dead – illustrating Hirst's title, "The Physical Impossibility of Death in the Mind of Someone Living."

Arguing it out

Modern art can provoke fierce arguments and sometimes even court cases. Everyone has different ideas and opinions, and it is no easy matter to resolve them. Sculptor Constantin Brancusi sued U.S. Customs to prove his sculptures were "art." He won; but artist Richard Serra wasn't so lucky. He made a huge, curving wall of steel entitled *Tilted Arc* for a New York square. The arc angered locals, who said it kept them from using the square. For Serra, that was the point – he wanted to change their awareness of space. But, after a court hearing, judges ordered that it be removed.

In 1998-99, Tracey Emin sparked off a huge controversy by exhibiting her own bed as art. Two visiting artists were even inspired to stage a pillow fight on it in protest.

Looking at modern art

Many people find modern art baffling, especially if they expect to recognize what they see, or are looking for traditional skills such as being able to draw accurately from life. But there are lots of other ways to think about art. These pages explain some of the questions you could ask when looking at it.

👁 For links to websites where you can view a selection of modern art or take an online "art safari," go to **www.usborne-quicklinks.com**

What's it all about?

One of the most puzzling things about modern art is that it is not always obvious what it's really about. But the title may give you a clue – even if it is just *Composition* or *Improvisation*. Vague titles often mean the artist wasn't trying to show a particular scene, but to explore his or her ideas about art or life.

There will also be clues in the work itself – even if they may be hard to spot at first. Look at it carefully and think about what the image shows, and the style and colors the artist used, and how they make you feel.

Some paintings and sculptures don't have clear subjects. They use colors and shapes for artistic effect, rather than as a way of representing scenes. This is known as abstract art. You are meant to appreciate these works as things in their own right, not as images of something else.

The Snail (1953), by Henri Matisse; gouache on cut and pasted paper, 113 x 113in. At first glance, this just seems like a bright, cheerful pattern. But the title suggests there is more to it. Do you think the spiraling arrangement resembles the spiral shape of a snail shell? There is also a tiny snail silhouette jutting out of the lilac shape in the corner.

How was it made?

It is worth thinking about how something was made, too. Modern artists don't just paint and sculpt, they use a huge range of materials or "media." Some make films or photographs, or work with things they happen to find. Others design works for specific places – these are known as "installations." And some artists don't actually make things at all, but put on shows or document their thoughts. Their choice of methods will depend a lot on their ideas about art.

Untitled (1985), by Donald Judd; painted aluminum, 12 x 47 x 12in. Judd used metal and other industrial materials because he wanted to explore their particular qualities.

When was it made?

If you know something about when a work of art was made, and what else was happening at the time, it may help to explain why an artist chose to work in a certain way. Big historic events such as wars affect everyone, including artists. And the development of art movements such as Cubism or Impressionism, when artists work together and share ideas, can greatly influence an individual artist's style. But it is misleading to see things just in terms of "isms." Art doesn't fit neatly into categories. Each artist and each work is different.

Girl with a Kitten (1947), by Lucian Freud; oil on canvas, 16 x 12in. Freud is known for painting intense, detailed portraits. But it is hard to categorize his style, which is sometimes compared to Realism, sometimes to Expressionism.

Do you like it?

Another important question is whether you like a work of art or not, and why. There are no right or wrong answers to this question. It is a matter of taste – and tastes change. What seemed shocking a hundred years ago may look ordinary today. The Impressionists were considered outrageous in the 1850s. But now they are greatly admired. Compared to a lot of very recent art, they even seem fairly traditional.

About this book

This book traces the history of modern art, from the 1850s to the present day. It is arranged roughly in the order things happened, so you can see how different kinds of art developed, and how they related to events at the time. Each section covers a major period of art history, introduces its main ideas and movements, and looks at a few important works in more depth. If you can, try to visit an art gallery or museum too, so you can experience the impact of seeing art first-hand. You can also see a lot more art on the internet – look out for the recommended websites throughout this book.

Maman (1999), by Louise Bourgeois; bronze and steel, 365 x 351 x 403in. This huge spider is just one example of what you can see at art museums. It stands outside the Guggenheim Museum in Bilbao, Spain.

BREAKING AWAY

During the 19th century, many artists broke with tradition and began to explore radical new ideas and ways of making art. This trend is often described as the rise of the *avant-garde* – a French term which originally meant the advance unit of an army. Now, it has come to mean innovative, cutting-edge art.

Detail from *Street with Prostitutes* (1914-25), by Ernst Kirchner. You can see the whole picture on page 21.

Making a big impression

For centuries, most artists worked hard to create highly polished, lifelike paintings, often with serious historic or religious themes. Then, in the 1870s, a group of young French artists began showing pictures of ordinary, everyday scenes painted in a fluid, unfinished-looking style. Much of the art world was horrified. These rebellious artists – now known as the Impressionists – formed the first avant-garde art movement.

Out and about

In the past, artists had mostly worked in studios. But, in the 1860s, some young art students, including Claude Monet and Pierre-Auguste Renoir, began to paint outdoors. They did this because they felt it made their pictures seem fresher and more immediate. They were also taking advantage of new art equipment, such as portable tubes of paint. Artists had always gone on painting trips, but only to make studies for paintings they completed later, back in the studio. Compared to studio art, the students' pictures looked very rough and sketchy, painted with rapid strokes of almost unblended color. But Monet and the others took the radical step of presenting these pictures as finished works of art.

The Swing (1876), by Pierre-Auguste Renoir; oil on canvas, 36 x 29in. Notice the bright dabs of paint that Renoir used to suggest the dappled effect of sunlight shining through the trees.

Impression: Sunrise (1872), by Claude Monet; oil on canvas, 19 x 24in

Light and shade

Monet and his friends wanted to explore the constantly changing effects of natural light. *Impression: Sunrise* is one early example, a study of dawn light on misty air and water. Its title led the art critic Louis Leroy to dub the new style "Impressionism." But Leroy meant it as an insult, saying that wallpaper designers did better work!

Impression: Sunrise shows the French port of Le Havre, but you can barely make out the boats. Monet was more interested in the effect of the orange sun and purplish haze.

Monet once had the spring leaves removed from some trees, so he could finish doing a winter scene.

Mad artists

The Impressionists turned their attention to the city as well as the countryside, painting busy streets, cafés, parks and stations. This might not seem remarkable now. But, at the time, it was unusual for artists to focus on scenes of everyday life, like the Paris street on the right, or ordinary people, as in the drawing below.

Although the Impressionists are very popular now, they got a hostile reaction to begin with. The group's work was rejected by all the official exhibitions, so they had to organize their own shows. They were also ridiculed in the press. After their 1876 show, a reviewer called them "lunatics."

The Boulevard Montmartre at Night (1897), by Camille Pissarro; oil on canvas, 21 x 26in. Pissarro did a whole series of paintings of this view at different times of day. This version shows it on a dark, rainy night, lit by the artificial glow of streetlamps and shop windows. See how the light seems to shimmer off the wet street, drawing your eye across the surface of the picture.

Women on the Terrace of a Café (1877), by Edgar Degas; pastel on paper, 17 x 22in. Notice how the women at the edges are partly cut off, as they would be in a photo. The arrangement is very different from the careful poses of traditional paintings.

For links to websites where you can find out all about Impressionism and create your own masterpiece, go to **www.usborne-quicklinks.com**

Capturing the moment

Although photography was only invented in the 1830s, by the time of the Impressionists it was fairly widespread. This meant many artists felt they no longer needed to create realistic images – the camera could do that instead. But they did use photos to study movement, looking at motion frame by frame. Photos influenced the composition of pictures, too. Artists began to sketch more informal views, from unexpected angles, as if they were taking snapshots. This helped make their pictures feel more spontaneous, giving them a natural appearance, as if done on the spot.

Colorful views

Toward the end of the 19th century, some artists thought up startling and original ways of using color. Some wanted to exploit new scientific theories about how we see color. Others began choosing colors for their symbolic or emotional associations, trying to make their pictures bolder and brighter and even more expressive than life.

A Sunday on La Grande Jatte (1884-86), by French artist Georges Seurat; oil on canvas, 81 x 120in

Making a point

In the 1880s, Georges Seurat invented a technique known as "Pointillism," using tiny dots of pure, contrasting colors. The scene above contains about 3.5 million dots. Seen from a distance, the dots blur, so the colors seem to blend together. Seurat was inspired by new research into the science of optics – how we see things, especially color. He thought that letting colors mix in the eye, rather than on his palette, made them appear brighter and richer.

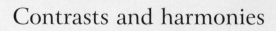

You can see the individual dots
more clearly in this enlarged detail.

Contrasts and harmonies

Seurat designed his dots to exploit the way colors are affected by the other colors around them. For example, blue contrasts most strongly with orange, so blue looks brighter next to orange. You can use a "color wheel" to work out these contrasts. In the wheel, each color lies opposite its "complementary" color, the color it contrasts with most intensely. It sits next to its "harmonizing" colors – the colors most similar to it.

The color wheel contains red, yellow and
blue, and the colors you get by mixing them.

Sunshine and flowers

In 1888, Dutch artist Vincent van Gogh moved to Arles, in the south of France. Inspired by the sun-drenched southern landscape, he began to use brighter, sunnier colors in his paintings. After a few months, his friend Paul Gauguin came to live and work with him.

Sunflowers grew all around Arles, and van Gogh did a series of sunflower pictures to decorate the house and welcome Gauguin. Van Gogh loved these brilliant yellow flowers, which he sketched rapidly in thick, bumpy layers of paint. New "chrome" yellows – bright, chemical-based colors – had recently become available, and van Gogh used them almost undiluted. He thought colors had symbolic values and, for him, these yellows represented happiness, friendship and harmony – as well as dazzling the viewer.

Sunflowers (1888), by Vincent van Gogh; oil on canvas, 36 x 29in. Notice the touches of blue on the vase and table. They make the orangey-yellows beside them stand out even more.

Island dreams

Gauguin and van Gogh worked closely together, but in very different styles. Van Gogh liked painting from life, while Gauguin preferred to follow his imagination, often choosing spiritual themes. His pictures are much smoother and flatter, with more simplified shapes. But both artists exaggerated colors, and Gauguin encouraged others to do the same. He claimed color was the most important part of a painting.

The partnership in Arles lasted until the winter, when the friends began to fall out. After a violent quarrel, Gauguin fled. A few years later, he left France entirely, in search of an earthly paradise. He traveled to Tahiti, in the South Pacific, where he made many paintings and carvings inspired by the vivid scenery and ancient religious myths he found there.

She is Called Vairaumati (1892), by Paul Gauguin; oil on canvas, 36 x 27in. According to Tahitian myth, Vairaumati was a great beauty who became the wife of the Tahitian god, Oro.

👁 For links to websites where you can find out more about these artists and about how artists use color, go to **www.usborne-quicklinks.com**

The Starry Night

This dramatic night scene, with twinkling stars and twisting, inky skies, is one of the best-known works by famous Dutch artist, Vincent van Gogh. "Looking at the stars always makes me dream," he said, and this scene is one of the few landscapes he painted indoors, from imagination and memory.

Title: *The Starry Night*
Date: 1889
Artist: Vincent van Gogh
Materials: oil on canvas
Size: 29 x 36in

Real and imagined

The Starry Night shows a landscape dominated by a swirling night sky and flame-like cypress trees. The sky itself was based on the view from van Gogh's window in France, where he was living, but he made up the village with its Dutch-style church. The neat, straight lines of the houses contrast dramatically with the swirls and curls of their surroundings.

Star-gazing

According to astronomers, van Gogh's night sky is fairly accurate, with the bright star Venus low over the horizon. But van Gogh may have chosen to paint exactly eleven stars because of the Bible story about Joseph. Dreaming of a brilliant future, Joseph says: "Behold... the sun and the moon and the eleven stars made obeisance to me" (meaning they bowed to him).

Express yourself

Van Gogh liked to use strong colors, often straight from the tube, and applied his paint very thickly, leaving obvious brushmarks. Because he suffered from mental illness – which at one point drove him to cut off part of his left ear – many people think his striking colors and rough, restless brushstrokes are the result of a tormented mind. And there is certainly something turbulent about *The Starry Night*, which was painted while the artist was staying at a mental hospital in Saint-Rémy, France.

But, in spite of the traumas of mental breakdown, van Gogh was able to exert great control and skill in his art. He used color and texture very deliberately, to create a heightened emotional effect. "Instead of trying to reproduce exactly what I have before my eyes," he wrote, "I use color arbitrarily, in order to express myself more forcibly." His expressive, individual style had a great influence on modern art, especially on the movement which became known as Expressionism.

In this close-up of the picture surface, you can clearly see the lines in the paint left by van Gogh's brush. A thick layer of paint like this is known as *impasto*, from the Italian word for "paste."

For a link to a website where you can see all the paintings and drawings van Gogh made during his life, go to **www.usborne-quicklinks.com**

About van Gogh

Van Gogh was a preacher's son, born in Holland in 1853. He tried several jobs before becoming an artist, working as a picture dealer, teacher and lay preacher. In 1880, he decided to devote himself to art. From then until his death, he worked relentlessly, producing over 2000 drawings and paintings in ten years. He committed suicide in 1890.

Although van Gogh's paintings are famous today, they were not very popular in his own time. Even his friends said they looked like the work of a madman. He sold only one painting during his life, and had to rely on his brother, Theo, for support. Yet, in 1990, his painting *Portrait of Dr. Gachet* smashed art-market records when it sold at auction for $82.5 million.

Self Portrait (1889), by Vincent van Gogh; oil on canvas, 26 x 21in. Van Gogh painted this in Saint-Rémy, just a few months after *The Starry Night*.

Running wild

As artists continued to experiment with color, they began to produce paintings that were more vibrant, and less lifelike, than any before. Instead of trying to imitate nature – which seemed less important now photography had been invented – they began to think about what makes a strong picture in its own right. They believed this would help them create more original, imaginative works of art.

Painting lessons

Among the artists exploring new approaches to painting was a group named the Nabis, or "prophets" in Hebrew. They were strongly influenced by Gauguin, who encouraged them to use intense, undiluted colors. Paul Sérusier painted the woodland scene on the right during a lesson with Gauguin. In fact, it looks more like a pattern of colored shapes than a picture of a real wood. It illustrates one of the ideas of the Nabis: "A painting... is essentially a flat surface with colors organized in a certain order."

The Talisman (1888), by Paul Sérusier; oil on wood, 11 x 9in. Can you make out trees with blue trunks?

Henri Matisse (1905), by André Derain; oil on canvas, 18 x 14in. Notice how the bluish shadows on the face are offset by patches of orange (the complementary of blue) around the eyes.

Wild beasts

In 1905, French artists Henri Matisse and André Derain spent the summer at Collioure, a small port in southern France. Here, they painted each other's portraits – you can see Derain's one of Matisse on the left – and other scenes, experimenting with bright, pure colors. Like the Nabis, they didn't think colors had to be lifelike. And they didn't want to weaken the effect by blending them. So they chose the most vivid colors and applied them in solid patches. The result can seem crude, but it is actually a careful balance of complementary colors (see page 14).

When some of the friends' work went on show in Paris that fall, along with similarly colorful pictures by Maurice Vlaminck and a few others, the public greeted it with shock and outrage. One critic thought it looked so wild, he nicknamed the whole group *Fauves*, French for "Wild Beasts." He meant it as an insult, but the name stuck, and it is still how they are known today.

Open Window, Collioure (1905), by Henri Matisse; oil on canvas, 22 x 18in. Notice how the wall is a very different color on each side of the window – an effect which could be created by strong sun on one side, and shade on the other.

Matisse thought art should be pleasant and soothing. He said he wanted: "an art of purity and serenity... something like a good armchair that provides relaxation from fatigue."

Sun, sand and sea

The sunny sea view above was painted in Collioure by Matisse. It shows French windows opening onto a little balcony, neatly framing the boats drawn up on the beach beyond. Everything is loosely sketched in dazzling hues, with almost no shading. It is meant to be a celebration of color, not a slavish imitation of real life – though it does give a very real sense of what it is like to look out at such a bright, sunlit landscape.

The open window helps create a sense of space. It also frames the boats like a picture within the picture. Matisse may have meant this to draw attention to the process of picture-making itself, which he was completely revolutionizing.

Warm and cool

Matisse's sea view is built up of colors rather than solid, 3-D shapes. He used the contrast between warm and cool colors to structure his painting, doing the sunny parts in bright, warm reds, pinks and oranges, and the shady areas in cool blues and greens. Matisse said: "When I put a green, it is not grass. When I put a blue, it is not the sky." He was inspired by the intensity and contrasts of the colors themselves as much as by the scene itself.

For links to websites where you can explore a virtual exhibition all about the Fauves or create your own Matisse picture, go to **www.usborne-quicklinks.com**

Express yourself

In the early years of the 20th century, many artists began to search for more expressive ways of painting. Instead of focusing on how things looked, they wanted to explore the vast territory of human emotions. So they began to heighten colors and exaggerate shapes to communicate strong feelings, from joy to despair. This became known as Expressionism.

Screaming out

Expressionism was heavily influenced by the work of two artists: Vincent van Gogh and Norwegian artist, Edvard Munch. Munch made many paintings about sickness, death and loneliness. He said he wanted his work to show "living beings who breathe and feel and love and suffer," as he must have done. His mother and sister died tragically young from TB, and he himself was often ill.

The Scream is one of the most famous Expressionist images. Munch did several versions of it, ranging from bright, jarring oil paintings to bleak, black and white prints, like the one here. It shows a haggard figure standing on a bridge in a swirling landscape. He seems to be clutching his head in pain, as if trapped in a state of anguish, surrounded by a silent but still reverberating scream.

The Scream (1895), by Edvard Munch; lithograph, 14 x 10in. Munch said this image was inspired by a walk he took, when he felt "an endless scream passing through nature."

Reclining Woman with Green Stockings (1917), by Egon Schiele; gouache and black crayon on paper, 12 x 18in. Notice the model's odd, contorted pose and the way she stares directly at us – unlike traditional paintings, which usually show women looking away.

Separate agenda

In Germany and Austria, Expressionism was taken up by groups of rebellious artists who cut themselves off from traditional art academies. Their breakaway movement became known as the Secession. In Vienna, the Secession was led by Gustav Klimt, and he encouraged Egon Schiele to join too. Schiele did many drawings of nude or scantily clad models. Instead of trying to make them appear demure and seductive, as a traditional artist might, he used rough lines and bruised colors to create awkward, tormented images, full of sexual tension and even aggression.

Building bridges

In 1905, four young German artists – Ernst Kirchner, Karl Schmidt-Rottluff, Fritz Bleyl and Eric Heckel – founded a group named *Die Brücke*, which is German for "The Bridge." They wanted to create a bridge to the future, to a new kind of art. Inspired by both African and medieval European art, they used bold, angular shapes and bright, unnatural colors – as in this Berlin street scene by Kirchner.

Kirchner made a series of paintings about the seedy side of life in Berlin. The two women in this picture are probably prostitutes. The men on the sidewalk eye the woman in red, their faces like sickly, green masks. And the odd perspective makes the ground seem to tilt precariously. The effect is to make a busy, everyday street seem strange and unsafe. Kirchner may have been expressing the unease of a nation on the brink of war – he made this painting shortly before the outbreak of the First World War.

Street with Prostitutes (1914-25), by Ernst Kirchner; oil on canvas, 49 x 36in. Notice the blue, watery color of the street, which makes it look more like a river than a roadway.

Horsing around

Another Expressionist group was set up in Germany in 1911, by Franz Marc and Vassily Kandinsky. They named it *Der Blaue Reiter*, German for "The Blue Rider" – which was also the name of a painting by Kandinsky and a journal they published in 1912.

The Blue Rider artists believed art should focus on spiritual ideas. Marc specialized in painting animals, especially horses, because for him they symbolized a better way of life. He thought they were more in harmony with the world around them than people.

Stables (1913), by Franz Marc; oil on canvas, 29 x 62in. The smooth shapes of the horses are broken by the lines of the stables.

Seeing things differently

Ever since the 15th century, most artists had used a system of rules known as perspective to create the illusion of showing people and objects as if in real or 3-D space.

But, in the late 19th and early 20th centuries, some artists began to experiment with different ways of seeing things – with some startling results.

Left: *Still Life with Basket* (1888-90), by French painter Paul Cézanne; oil on canvas, 26 x 32in

Right: *Fruit* (1820), by American still life artist James Peale; oil on canvas, 17 x 27in

Getting it in perspective

Fruit, by James Peale – who specialized in very lifelike still lifes – follows the rules of perspective. Each object is painted with great detail and accuracy, and is the right size and shape in relation to all the others. Everything is seen from a single viewpoint, as if we were standing motionless by the table. By contrast, Paul Cézanne's picture looks roughly painted and full of distortions.

Different angles

To show things in perspective, artists have to draw everything from the same viewpoint. But Cézanne thought that didn't reflect how we really see the world. After all, few people would stare at a table for hours without moving. He wanted to find a new way of representing space. So he began painting scenes from different angles, combining several viewpoints in one picture.

Still Life with Basket shows a clay jar, seen from above, next to a china pot which has been drawn side-on. The left and right-hand sections of the table don't line up, and the basket balances impossibly on the edge. The shifting perspective makes the scene seem disjointed – but perhaps it is closer to how you would see things if you were walking around the room yourself?

Cézanne was obsessed with still lifes like this, painting the same objects over and over again. He would spend hours creating each arrangement, propping things up on piles of coins, and soaking cloths in plaster so they folded just the way he wanted.

Bits and pieces

After Cézanne died, there was a big memorial exhibition of his work in Paris. Its visitors included two young artists, Pablo Picasso and Georges Braque. Inspired by Cézanne, they too began to experiment with perspective. But they went even further and gave up trying to create any illusion of space altogether. Instead, they combined bits and pieces seen from different angles or at different times, and broke up the surfaces of their pictures with geometric shapes. In this way, they hoped to highlight the contradictions involved in trying to paint solid-looking, 3-D objects on a flat, 2-D surface. This new approach became known as Cubism.

Looking for clues

At first glance, it's hard to make out anything in the jumble of shapes on the right. But on closer inspection it's full of clues. Near the top is a rectangular bottle-shape, faintly labeled "RHU" – the beginning of *rhum*, French for "rum." Behind it lies a clarinet, its finger holes seen from the side, but its flared end shown from above. There are also several curly shapes, such as musical clefs, and the word *valse*, French for "waltz," suggesting sheet music. And, near the bottom, can you spot a square fireplace arch and a decorative scroll of the sort you might find carved on a mantelpiece?

Clarinet and Bottle of Rum on a Mantelpiece (1911), by Georges Braque; oil on canvas, 32 x 24in. Can you spot a pin-shape about a third of the way down, slightly to the right of the center? It has a shadow that makes it seem to stick right out of the painting – an ironic 3-D touch in an otherwise flat, 2-D picture.

Sticky business

From 1912, Picasso and Braque did something no "painter" had done before. They began to glue pieces of paper and cloth onto their pictures. This method became known as collage, from the French *coller,* meaning "to stick." It was the beginning of a new kind of art known as assemblage, where whole works are "assembled" from bits of different materials.

Still Life with Chair Caning shows a group of objects on a cane chair seat, framed with rope. The objects are painted in a fragmentary, Cubist style, but the seat is actually a piece of cloth printed with a canework pattern. The mixture of materials and techniques blurs the boundaries between real objects, such as the cloth, and painted ones, such as the glass. Picasso did this to make us question the relationship between art and reality.

Still Life with Chair Caning (1912), by Pablo Picasso; oil and oilcloth on canvas with rope frame, 11 x 14in. From left to right, the objects shown are: a newspaper with the letters "JOU," a clay pipe, a goblet of beer and a knife slicing a piece of fruit.

Les Demoiselles

In 1907, Picasso completed his experimental painting *Les Demoiselles d'Avignon* – to the horror of most people who saw it. Even the artist's friends were upset by its crude, harsh style. So he left it rolled up in his studio for years. But it went on display eventually, first in Paris and then New York. Today, it is one of the most famous paintings in the world.

Title: *Les Demoiselles d'Avignon*
Date: 1907
Artist: Pablo Picasso
Materials: oil on canvas
Size: 96 x 92in

Art experiments

Picasso painted *Les Demoiselles d'Avignon* as he and Braque began to experiment with Cubism. They were trying to leave behind traditional ideas about beauty and perspective. So Picasso used glaring colors and jagged shapes, set at odd angles. Everything is fragmented, from the women themselves to the spaces between them, making what should be a 3-D scene appear disjointed and flat.

Changing faces

The women on the left of the painting were probably inspired by ancient Spanish statues. They look very different from the women on the right, whose faces resemble African masks. The clash of styles makes the picture feel even more disjointed and disturbing. In fact, Picasso originally gave all the women similar faces. But he was suddenly inspired to repaint the two on the right after seeing displays of African art in Paris. By using non-Western art as a source, he hoped to bypass the history of Western painting and go back to something older and more primitive.

Picasso wrestled with the composition, doing over a hundred preparatory sketches. Early versions included two men, a sailor and a student holding a book or skull. The sailor was probably meant to represent desire, and the student, knowledge. And skulls are a traditional symbol of death. So Picasso may have been thinking of the moral, "the wages of sin are death." But in the end he left out the men and created a less symbolic, more ambiguous composition.

Picasso worked in many different art forms throughout his life. This photograph, taken in 1948, shows him painting a design onto a plate.

Ladies of the night

Les Demoiselles d'Avignon is French for "ladies of Avignon." Avignon was the name of a street in the red-light district of Barcelona, where Picasso grew up. So these women are meant to be prostitutes, posing to seduce their clients. But they don't look very attractive. Picasso gave them lopsided, angular bodies, with staring eyes or threatening-looking masks, perhaps reflecting fears of his own about sexuality.

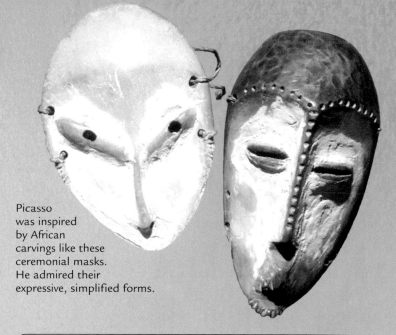

Picasso was inspired by African carvings like these ceremonial masks. He admired their expressive, simplified forms.

Picasso had a long and successful artistic career. For a link to a website where you can explore his life's work, go to **www.usborne-quicklinks.com**

Beyond Cubism

Picasso is probably the most famous modern artist – he was certainly one of the most prolific and varied. He produced an amazing 22,000 works, from portraits, political art, prints and illustrations to sculptures, set designs and ceramics. His early works were atmospheric, delicately colored paintings. Art historians often divide these into a "blue" and a "rose" period, because of the way his use of color changed. Then, he experimented with Cubism and Surrealism. His energy and talent meant he was able to paint in almost any style he wanted.

Bright lights, big city

As the 20th century progressed, cities continued to expand rapidly – and so too did the number of artists who took city life as their subject. But they painted it in very different ways – from shifting Cubist perspectives to a hard-edged precision that seemed well-suited to the new machine age.

City living

French artist Robert Delaunay lived in Paris and did many paintings of the city. Often, he deliberately included symbols of the exciting new age, such as the plane, invented only a few years before, or the Eiffel Tower, then the world's tallest building. *The Red Tower* shows the Eiffel Tower caught between apartment blocks, early high-rise buildings which soon came to symbolize modern urban life. In fact, it is less one view than a series of glances. Delaunay used multiple views to make it feel as if the viewer is actually on the move, caught up in the speed and bustle of the city.

The Red Tower (1911-12), by Robert Delaunay; oil on canvas, 64 x 51in. Shifting angles create a dizzying sense of height.

Caught up in the crowd

As cities grew, so did the crowds of people thronging their streets. British painter and writer Percy Wyndham Lewis was fascinated by the behavior of crowds, and their effect on politics. In *The Crowd*, he shows groups of stick-like figures, gathering in a maze of streets between angular buildings. They seem to be led by men with red Communist flags. There is also a *tricolore*, the French national flag, in one corner. So perhaps the scene is meant to evoke the thrill – or danger – of mass political protests?

It's a blast

Wyndham Lewis helped found a movement known as Vorticism which celebrated modern life, machines and the city. The Vorticists published a magazine called *Blast* to publicize their ideas. In it, they demanded dramatic or even violent changes in British culture, and threatened to blast away everything which seemed old-fashioned.

The Crowd (1914-15), by Percy Wyndham Lewis; oil and pencil on canvas, 79 x 61in. This painting is also sometimes known as *Revolution*.

New York, New York

This atmospheric New York scene is by American painter Georgia O'Keeffe. It shows the 22-story Radiator Building, built just three years earlier and still a landmark in the city today. It was made of black brick with gold trimmings. But O'Keeffe shows it transformed by darkness into a neat pattern of light and dark, with bright white windows and a spotlit summit, and not a person in sight.

The picture is full of sharp lines and smooth shapes. Even the curling smoke on the right has a crisp edge. O'Keeffe liked to paint from life, but she concentrated on shapes so much, her work can seem almost abstract, conveying sensations as much as appearances. O'Keeffe was one of the pioneers of abstract art in America. She said: "One can't paint New York as it is, but rather as it is felt." Here, that feeling seems to be of a grand but rather daunting and impersonal beauty.

Radiator Building – Night, New York (1927), by Georgia O'Keeffe; oil on canvas, 48 x 30in. The word "Stieglitz" is just visible in the red neon sign. This was the name of O'Keeffe's husband, a famous photographer and art dealer.

👁 For links to websites where you can see more works by Delaunay or O'Keeffe, go to
www.usborne-quicklinks.com

The photograph below shows the New York skyline as it looks today. You can see how well O'Keeffe captured the pattern of light in the city's towering buildings.

Into the future

The early 20th century was a time of rapid changes, as more people began to live in bustling cities, work in industries driven by new machines, and travel ever faster by car or plane. In response, many artists began to make art about speed and machines, using experimental methods inspired by Cubism. Others turned their attention to the natural world, using similarly innovative techniques to capture the movement of animals.

For a link to a website where you can find out more about the Futurists and see many of their works, go to **www.usborne-quicklinks.com**

Time for a change

Some of the most dramatic changes took place in Italy, where new industries and a new political system were revolutionizing the country. Enthusiastic about modern ideas and the chance to remake their society, a group of Italian artists calling themselves "Futurists" set out to create a new art for the new age.

Futurist leader F.T. Marinetti even wanted to modernize Italian cooking by banning pasta, which he said was "a symbol of... dullness... and fat-bellied conceit."

In 1909, Italian poet F.T. Marinetti wrote a Futurist Manifesto setting out the movement's beliefs and aims. It declared the Futurists' love of fast movement and violent change, saying: "the world's splendor has been enriched by a new beauty, the beauty of speed."

Unique Forms of Continuity in Space (1913), by Futurist artist Umberto Boccioni; bronze, 46 x 35 x 15in. The flowing shapes are meant to convey forceful movement.

Out with the old

The Futurists wanted to destroy the past completely, saying people should burn down libraries and flood museums. Marinetti even went so far as to praise the destructiveness of war, calling it "the world's only hygiene." But when war actually came in 1914, the movement began to peter out, discredited by the horrors of real warfare and, later, by its links with Fascism.

Man and superman

Unique Forms shows a man striding forward energetically. But his movements have been exaggerated, turning his body into a series of strange, flowing forms. The streamlined edges and overlapping shapes suggest a muscular figure in motion. And the metallic finish makes him look like a powerful machine. The artist may have meant to show a kind of superior, strong man or "superman" described by philosopher Friedrich Nietzsche, and idealized by German and Italian Fascists.

Speeding along

Giacomo Ballà was a leading Futurist painter. Like Marinetti, he idolized the new, fast cars. In fact, their top speed wasn't very impressive by today's standards – only about 30mph – but it was faster than any vehicle had ever gone before. *Abstract Speed + Sound* is meant to show a red car roaring along a white road. The green and blue colors suggest the ground and sky, overlaid by geometric shapes designed to convey the noise and movement of the car. Ballà may have been inspired by the praise of cars in Marinetti's manifesto: "A racing car whose hood is adorned with great pipes, like snakes with explosive breath... is more beautiful than the *Victory of Samothrace*" (the name of a famous classical statue).

Abstract Speed + Sound (1913-14), by Giacomo Ballà; oil on board, 22 x 30in, including the frame. Notice how the image overflows onto the frame. A frame normally separates off a painting. But Ballà made his frame a continuation of the picture, making it feel closer to you.

Up, up and away

Romanian sculptor Constantin Brancusi was preoccupied by movement and especially flight. He made several abstracted sculptures of birds which he said tried to capture "the essence of flight." The shape on the right may not look like much like a bird. The body is incredibly long and smooth, with no wings or feathers. Even the head is only hinted at by a slanting oval at the top, ending in a beak-like point. But Brancusi wanted to focus on the bird's movement, not its appearance.

Brancusi thought that adding lots of lifelike details, such as wings or feathers, would distract the viewer and make his sculpture look static. So he created an evocative, streamlined shape which rises up from a narrow base, to make it look as if it were soaring up into the air – just like a bird in flight.

Bird in Space (1923), by Constantin Brancusi; brass, 57 x 7in. Brancusi made several versions of this sculpture, some in brass, some in marble, all carefully polished to create a perfectly smooth shape. When U.S. Customs refused to pass one of these *Bird in Space* sculptures as "art," Brancusi took them to court – and won.

Shapes and colors

In about 1910, artists began trying to create pictures which were not images of actual people or places or things, but "things" in their own right. So instead of painting recognizable scenes, they took the elements of painting – colors, lines and shapes – and put them together in expressive or evocative ways. This kind of art is known as abstract art, and many of its earliest pioneers were Russian.

Improvisation No. 26 (Rowing) (1912), by Vassily Kandinsky; oil on canvas, 38 x 43in. This picture is also sometimes known as *Oars*.

Kandinsky said he was inspired to try abstract art by seeing a painting which had fallen on its side. He thought the shapes in it looked more interesting upside down or sideways.

This abstract painting still contains traces of the scene which inspired it. Can you make out two figures in a red boat, grasping long, black lines which might be oars? The boat floats among dramatic splashes of color, suggesting a wild, watery setting. Above, a dark bird-like shape flies through an equally colorful sky.

Music and color

Vassily Kandinsky was a Russian painter who worked in Germany, where he founded the Blue Rider movement. But he was also a pioneer of abstract art, creating early, experimental works like *Rowing*. At first glance, this picture looks like an abstract, colorful pattern. In fact it was loosely based on a scene of two people in a boat. But when you look at it, you are aware of all the lines, shapes and colors as separate elements, rather than as ways of representing a scene. Kandinsky placed special emphasis on his use of color. He thought color could express feelings in the same way as music, claiming: "Color is a power that directly influences the soul... Color is the keyboard... The artist is the hand that plays."

Shaping up

Lyubov Popova was a leading Russian avant-garde artist. She experimented with Cubism and Futurism before going on to develop a more abstract style, setting simple geometric shapes against flat, plain backgrounds. Popova believed artists should not try to copy what they saw, but create their own vision instead. She wrote: "The representation of reality – without artistic deformation and transformation – cannot be the subject of painting."

But by the 1920s, in the aftermath of the Russian Revolution, Popova abandoned painting altogether, having decided that art should have a more practical purpose. So she joined a group known as the Constructivists and began to work on design projects, producing textiles, ceramics and posters.

👁 For links to websites where you can explore another abstract "improvisation" by Kandinksy, view one of Popova's geometric costume designs or discover lots more "Suprematist" compositions by Malevich, go to **www.usborne-quicklinks.com**

Untitled (1910), by Lyubov Popova; oil on canvas. This picture has been reduced to the simplest elements of painting.

Supreme artist

Russian painter Kasimir Malevich believed he could only really create art when he was making things up. He said: "the artist can be a creator only when the forms in his pictures have nothing in common with nature." So he began to create abstract images by painting plain, geometric shapes on square backgrounds. Using squares meant he could avoid traditional "landscape" or "portrait" formats, which might have made his pictures seem more like paintings of things, rather than things in themselves.

Malevich named the new style Suprematism, from the Latin *supremus*, meaning "of the highest order." He meant it to be a purer, more spiritual kind of art. After the Russian Revolution of 1917, he tried to promote abstract art as the right art for the radical new Russia. He didn't really convince the authorities – but he did have a great influence on other artists, including Kandinsky and Popova.

Dynamic Suprematism (1915-16), by Kasimir Malevich; oil on canvas, 31 x 31in. Malevich worried that simple abstract pictures could look static. So he began to use complicated arrangements of shapes, as in this composition, to try to create a sense of energetic or dynamic movement. He called this Dynamic Suprematism.

DREAMS & CONFLICTS

The 20th century was torn apart by two world wars, which had a huge impact on all aspects of life – including art. Artists' work changed, reflecting their shattered faith in new technologies, their distrust of a culture which could allow such things to happen, and the need to rebuild the world afterward.

Detail from *Travoys Arriving with Wounded at a Dressing Station at Smol, Macedonia 1916* (1919), by Stanley Spencer. You can see the whole picture on pages 36-37.

Going to war

Between 1914 and 1918, Europe was engulfed by the First World War. Millions were caught up in the conflict, including many artists – and many of them channeled their experiences into their art.

Often this resulted in striking pictures quite unlike traditional war paintings, which tend to concentrate on heroic battle scenes. The new images revealed a darker, more disturbing side of war.

Merry-Go-Round (1916), by Mark Gertler; oil on canvas, 75 x 56in. Gertler may have been inspired to paint this scene by a fair for wounded soldiers, held near his home in London.

Grim realities

The First World War was a different kind of conflict from earlier wars, fought with new and deadly weapons, such as planes, machine guns and poison gas. Some artists felt they needed to devise new ways of representing the horrors of mechanized warfare. Others thought only lifelike images could convey the grim realities of war.

Compare the painting on the left, by Mark Gertler, to the print on the right by Otto Dix. They look very different, but they are both about the war. Dix said, "One has to depict war realistically so it will be understood." But Gertler's picture doesn't do this. It uses a spinning carousel, painted in a smooth, almost mechanical-looking style, to symbolize the relentless progress of the war and its new machines.

👁 For a link to a website where you can see a huge selection of war art chosen to commemorate the First World War, go to **www.usborne-quicklinks.com**

Fairground horror

Merry-Go-Round shows men and women, some in military uniforms, sitting stiffly on an old-fashioned fairground carousel. They should be having fun. But the claustrophobic composition and bright, jarring colors make everything feel uneasy. And, if you look at the riders' faces, they seem to be screaming.

Gertler protested against the fighting, saying, "I just hate the war." So perhaps he did this painting to express his hatred. But, when the picture was first exhibited, reviewers thought it was just decorative. One even wrote that its style would be "admirably fitted for the adornment of a popular restaurant."

Casualties of war

German artist Otto Dix is famous for his pictures of social problems and war, reflecting his own experience of fighting and disillusionment afterward. The war haunted him, leaving him with recurring nightmares. After it ended, he published a series of 50 prints called *The War* – stark, black and white images of fierce fighting, mutilated bodies and devastated battlegrounds. The series was inspired by perhaps the greatest ever depiction of wartime atrocities, produced a century earlier by Spanish artist Francisco de Goya.

You can see one of Dix's prints below. It shows German troops, their faces hidden by alien-looking gas masks. They seem to be coming straight at us, one with his arm raised to hurl a grenade. The setting is dark and desolate, strewn with barbed wire and broken trees – a reminder of the destructiveness of war. It's a terrifying image. When it was first published, many Germans were shocked; they thought Dix should have made the soldiers look more heroic.

Disasters of War: The Same (1812-13), by Francisco de Goya; engraving, 6 x 9in. This is one of 80 prints Goya did evoking the horrors of the 1808-14 war between Spain and France.

The War: Assault under Gas (1924), by Otto Dix; engraving, 14 x 19in

Travoys Arriving

This painting by British artist Stanley Spencer shows wounded soldiers lying on travoys – stretchers pulled by mules – at a field hospital in Macedonia, in south-eastern Europe, during the First World War. Spencer worked as a medical orderly in Macedonia and later became a famous war artist. He was asked to paint this picture by the British government. It was the first painting he did after returning home from the war.

Title: *Travoys Arriving with Wounded at a Dressing Station at Smol, Macedonia 1916*
Date: 1919

Artist: Stanley Spencer
Materials: oil on canvas
Size: 72 x 86in

Casualties of war

The First World War was a bloody conflict, with huge casualties – over 8 million dead and 20 million wounded by the time it ended. Macedonia, on the war's southern front, saw fighting as bitter as anywhere. Spencer was sent there with the Royal Army Medical Corps in 1916. Years later, he described his experiences in a letter: "there were travoys and limbers crammed full of wounded men. One would have thought that the scene was... sordid... terrible... but I felt there was a grandeur."

Spencer had made sketches in Macedonia, but lost his sketchpad, so this scene was painted entirely from memory. The picture was meant for an official Hall of Remembrance. It doesn't commemorate an actual battle, but the quiet suffering of the wounded and the work of the medics caring for them. Although Spencer gave the picture a specific location, a place called Smol, the men could be any of the thousands caught up in the fighting. Their faces are all hidden, making the scene feel strangely impersonal. It also seems slightly unreal. The perspective has been distorted so things look strangely flat, and the colors and outlines have been simplified. This led critics at the time to compare Spencer with Cézanne and Picasso.

The dull brown and green color scheme makes everything seem bleak and somber. Even the plants in the corner look thorny and uncomfortable.

Religious echoes

The foreground is dominated by stretchers. But they point inward, making the brightly lit operating room the focus of attention. This composition, with the animals' heads silhouetted against the glowing interior, could even remind you of traditional nativity scenes.

Angels in sweaters

Spencer often combined ordinary details and religious imagery – as one critic at the time put it, "even his angels wear jumpers [sweaters]." Some of his best-known works show the Resurrection as described in the Bible, but set in his home village of Cookham. In *Travoys Arriving*, he said he wanted to create a peaceful, religious atmosphere, showing the soldiers like "so many crucified Christs" – reflecting their huge suffering, but also implying a hope that they would, like Christ, come back from the dead.

Salvation or suffering?

Is the painting really as peaceful and religious as Spencer claimed? There are no obvious religious references. Spencer supposedly based the hospital on one that had been set up in a ruined church, but there are no signs of church decor, and the only crosses are the red ones on the medics' armbands.

In fact, there is little hint of salvation – just a growing line of wounded men with no end in sight. More travoys are arriving from the right, and the wheel in the top right corner is a traditional symbol of a never-ending cycle of events. Perhaps Spencer found it hard to create a convincingly optimistic image. In 1919, the tragedy of the war was still fresh in people's minds – and the specter of a second world war was already beginning to loom.

A world gone crazy

During the First World War, some artists began to create deliberately strange, often shocking, works of art. Appalled by the fighting, they wanted to reject utterly the traditional values – cultural as well as political – which had allowed it to happen. So they made art using unconventional materials and methods, relying more on chance than artistic skill. They called this approach Dada – a deliberately meaningless title, chosen by just picking a word at random from a dictionary.

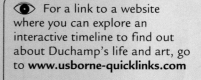

Fountain (1964, a replica of the original which was made in 1917 but later lost), by Marcel Duchamp; ceramic urinal, height 24in. The name "R. Mutt" is a variation of Mott, a French toilet manufacturer. But the signature was added by Duchamp.

Readymade art

One of the most famous Dada artworks ever made is Marcel Duchamp's *Fountain* – a urinal laid on its back and signed "R. Mutt, 1917." Duchamp referred to works which use manufactured objects like this as "readymades." By presenting a factory-made item as a work of art, Duchamp challenged the idea that art should be unique and produced by a skilled artist.

For Duchamp, an artist's ideas mattered more than his actual art. According to him, "Whether Mr. Mutt has made the fountain with his own hands or not is without importance. He chose it... he created a new thought for this object." But not everyone agreed. When Duchamp tried to exhibit *Fountain* at a show held by the Society of Independent Artists, they refused to let him, and he resigned from the society in protest.

👁 For a link to a website where you can explore an interactive timeline to find out about Duchamp's life and art, go to **www.usborne-quicklinks.com**

Putting on a show

Many people took refuge from the war in neutral Switzerland, especially in its biggest city, Zurich. Here, in 1916, Hugo Ball opened the Cabaret Voltaire, an evening show which quickly became an important Dada venue. He said the show's purpose was "to remind the world that there are people of independent minds, beyond war and nationalism" – although the owner of the cafe where it was held simply hoped it would help him sell more beer and sandwiches. At the shows, Ball and his friends staged bizarre acts – a kind of Performance art – in a room decorated with pictures by Hans Arp, Picasso and others. Ball himself dressed up and read "sound poems" composed of nonsense words. He felt he had to use made-up words because ordinary ones had become corrupt and meaningless.

At one Dada show, Hugo Ball put on a bright cardboard costume, with a tall hat, and solemnly chanted a poem full of words like "blago bung" and "ba-umf."

38

A load of old garbage

German Dada artist Kurt Schwitters made elaborate collages from garbage and the remnants of everyday life. The layers of the collages were a reflection of his own life, incorporating anything from newspapers he had read, to tickets for journeys he had made or shows he had seen. The example on the right includes an old bottle cork, scraps of wood, metal, paper and fabric, and a card with a printed picture of cherries, all carefully arranged into an abstract pattern of shapes and colors.

Schwitters coined the term "Merz" for his collage technique. The name came from one of his pictures where the end of the German word *kommerz*, or "commerce," was visible on a scrap of newspaper. Taking Merz to extremes, Schwitters filled whole rooms with huge, 3-D collages, trying to create a complete environment. He called these constructions *Merzbau*, or "Merz-buildings." While he was working on them, his friends said they would lose small items, such as keys and pencils, only to find them again later, built into his most recent construction.

Merz Picture 32A – Cherry Picture (1921), by Kurt Schwitters; collage of cloth, wood, metal, fabric, paper, cork, gouache, oil and ink on cardboard, 36 x 28in

Picture-traps

Dada had a huge influence on other artists over the following century, especially on a 1960s movement known as New Realism. The New Realists set out to explore modern life and consumer culture, often through works made of discarded items, from torn posters to old coffee grinders. By presenting them as art, these works questioned how things were produced and consumed in modern society. In some examples, known as *tableaux pièges* or "picture-traps," the artist "trapped" a chance collection of objects and hung them on the wall. These also "trap" the viewer by showing the unexpected – real, 3-D objects, instead of the 2-D painting you might expect to see.

Who knows where upstairs and downstairs are? (1964), by Daniel Spoerri; mixed media 3-D collage, 21 x 25 x 6in

In your dreams

In post-war Paris, a group of artists and writers, led by poet André Breton, began to create strange, dream-like works. They wanted to rebel against the rational, everyday world and, by drawing on their imagination and dreams, they hoped to create a new reality, or "surreality." Their movement became known as Surrealism.

More than real

Surrealism is known for its bizarre imagery, but it was not meant to be *un*-real. The name actually means *more* than real, or *sur*-real (*sur* is French for "above"). Breton said the movement rose from the ashes of Dada. It also grew out of a new interest in the workings of the mind, especially the irrational and the unconscious, inspired by turn-of-the-century Viennese psychiatrist Sigmund Freud. He claimed that much of what we do is triggered by unconscious thoughts and desires, and that these can be revealed in dreams.

The Surrealists believed the unconscious was the source of creative genius, and employed some unusual techniques to try to access it. Many tried "automatic" drawing, or drawing without thinking. They created strange, doodle-like pictures, which they believed were really shaped by their unconscious thoughts and impulses. Spanish painter Joan Miró even claimed to have starved himself to bring on hallucinations.

The Future of Statues (1937) by René Magritte; painted plaster, 13 x 7 x 8in

Strange meetings

The Surrealists loved new and startling combinations of things, seeing beauty in images such as "the chance encounter of an umbrella and a sewing machine on an operating table." They thought that these combinations reflected the way the unconscious could form associations and bring unconnected things together, which sometimes happens in dreams. Many bizarre Surrealist sculptures – which they called "objects" – were based on pairing unlikely items.

One of the most famous Surrealist objects was created when Salvador Dalí stuck a plaster lobster over the handset of a telephone.

Light and air

Belgian Surrealist René Magritte often created poetic, disturbing images by painting ordinary things in new and unexpected places. For example, *The Future of Statues* is a human head painted over with a blue sky full of drifting clouds. The sky makes the head seem dreamy and insubstantial, as if it were dissolving into air. Perhaps this dissolving is the "future of statues," which must eventually crumble away?

The head is actually a replica of the Emperor Napoleon's death mask – a cast of his face made after he died. So the sculpture may be meant to refer to human mortality, too. And it is a tribute to the power of the imagination, a visual pun on the idea of a daydreamer with his "head in the clouds."

Dream photography

The Persistence of Memory, by Spanish Surrealist Salvador Dalí, shows a golden landscape dominated by drooping watches and a misshapen, fleshy creature lying on the ground. Three of the watches are melting, while the case of a fourth watch is crawling with ants, as if it is being eaten. The hard, mechanical watches are soft and decaying, no longer able to measure the passage of time. The cliffs in the distance are actually based on the coast of Catalonia, where Dalí grew up – so perhaps the title was meant to refer to the artist's childhood memories. Ants were a childhood phobia of his. And the creature in the middle is actually a distorted version of his own profile, its long-lashed eye shut as if he is asleep or dead, unaware of, or out of, time.

The mysterious, dream-like imagery makes this a very strange scene. But Dalí painted it so realistically that it almost looks photographic – in fact, he called his works "hand-painted dream photographs." By presenting an imaginary scene in such a lifelike way, he intended to blur the boundary between imagination and reality. He said he wanted his paintings to spread confusion, in order to "discredit completely the world of reality."

Dalí was probably the most famous of all the Surrealists. By the end of his life, his face was so well-known that a letter could reach him addressed only with a drawing of his trademark moustache and the word *España* (Spain).

The Persistence of Memory (1931) by Salvador Dalí; oil on canvas, 10 x 13in. This is just one example of what Dalí called his "deceptive, hyper-normal and sickly images of concrete irrationality."

For a link to a website where you can see more of Dalí's paintings, go to **www.usborne-quicklinks.com**

Building the future

In the years following the First World War, there was a need to rebuild countries devastated by conflict, and many artists became involved with architecture and design. By integrating art with their surroundings, they hoped to create a better world for everyone. This resulted in several influential, idealistic art and design movements: Constructivism in Russia, De Stijl in Holland and Bauhaus in Germany.

Constructing art

Constructivism emerged after the Russian Revolution of 1917. The artists who joined the movement wanted to invent a more accessible kind of art for the people of the new Communist state. They tried to develop a fresh approach based on abstract, geometric forms, which they hoped would appeal to everyone, whatever their background.

As their name suggests, the Constructivists also wanted to use their art to build things – although a lot of their ideas never made it off the drawing board. Their slogan was "Art into Life." Many of them worked for the Communist government, designing propaganda posters, clothes, dishes, furniture, buildings and books. But, after Stalin took over, their style fell out of fashion. The leader of the new regime preferred art that showed actual people, generally workers in heroic poses – this style became known as Soviet Socialist Realism. Constructivism was suppressed and many of its most successful artists left Russia.

Oval Hanging Construction Number 12 (1920), by Alexander Rodchenko; plywood, aluminum paint and wire, 24 x 33 x 19in. Rodchenko made a series of constructions, but only this one survives. It consists of a flat oval, divided into sections that can be opened up. It was meant to be hung from the ceiling like a mobile.

In 1919-20, Vladimir Tatlin built a huge model showing his plans for a *Monument to the Third International* – a tower to commemorate the Third International Communist Congress, held in Moscow in 1921. But the design never got beyond the model stage.

Towering high

One of the most famous examples of Constructivist design was Vladimir Tatlin's *Monument to the Third International* – even though the monument itself was never actually built. Tatlin wanted it to be the tallest building in the world, a 1,300ft spiraling tower of metal and glass. Inside, there were to be three geometric blocks of office space: a cube at the bottom, a cone in the middle, and a cylinder near the top, all rotating at different speeds. Even with modern engineering, it would probably be impossible to build a structure like this. But the Constructivists wanted to push ideas to their limits.

Setting the style

De Stijl is Dutch for "The Style." This was the title of an art magazine founded in 1917 by Theo van Doesburg, as well as the name of the movement he led with Piet Mondrian. They wanted to create a pure, simple kind of art, using geometric forms and the primary colors – red, yellow and blue. Mondrian made whole pictures based on opposing horizontal and vertical lines, reflecting his belief that the universe was built on opposites. He was so strict about this, he left De Stijl when van Doesburg began to use diagonal lines. The members of De Stijl applied their pared-down style to design and architecture, creating striking, modern-looking furniture, interiors and buildings, as well as abstract paintings. They wanted to combine all the arts to create a harmonious, well-ordered environment. But not everyone liked the results. Van Doesburg's radical designs for the "Café d'Aubette" cinema-dance hall in Strasbourg proved unpopular with visitors and were quickly changed.

Colour Scheme for the Café d'Aubette Ballroom (1927), by Theo van Doesburg; ink and gouache on paper, 21 x 15in. For van Doesburg, the Café was one of the greatest De Stijl achievements and he dedicated a whole issue of his magazine to it.

House of building

De Stijl had a great influence in Germany where, in 1919, architect Walter Gropius set up an art school known as Bauhaus – which means "house of building" in German. Students at the school studied painting and design, along with craft skills such as woodwork and pottery. In this way, Gropius hoped to blur the traditional distinction between arts and crafts. He wanted his students to create objects that were both stylish and practical. He also encouraged them to learn about industrial processes, to help them design items for mass production. Bauhaus designs proved very popular. But its courses were too radical for the Nazis, who feared the school would corrupt its students and forced it to close in 1933. Many of its teachers left Germany, helping to spread Bauhaus ideas abroad – particularly in America, where many of them went on to have successful careers.

● For links to websites where you can see pictures of many Constructivist designs and artworks, go to **www.usborne-quicklinks.com**

This photo shows the Bauhaus building in Dessau – the school was originally based in Weimar, but moved here in 1926. This building was built to Gropius' own plans. At the time, its plain, functional design was very unusual and greatly admired.

The power of persuasion

For a long time, artists and governments have used art as a form of protest or propaganda, to try to shape people's ideas. Especially potent images were created in the 1930s, as the Nazi party rose to power in Germany. Anti-Nazi artists attacked the new regime, while the Nazis tried to suppress this art and promote their own instead.

Happy families

In the 1930s, the Nazis mounted a huge campaign against what they called "degenerate" art, by which they meant all radical art, because they thought it was subversive. Nazi leader Adolf Hitler, himself a failed artist, hated a lot of art, particularly Expressionism. He wanted art to be "the messenger of noble and beautiful things" – not to examine difficult emotions or social problems. *Family Portrait* is an example of the kind of art he liked.

At first sight, this painting looks like an innocent family scene. But it was designed to promote Nazi ideas. The blond, blue-eyed figures represent Hitler's ideal Aryan, or pure-blooded, Germans. The nursing mother reinforces Nazi ideas about the proper role of women. And the pretty setting, with the family surrounded by the produce of a well-tended garden, reflects the Nazis' belief in the importance of land. They used a need for land as an excuse to invade neighboring countries.

Family Portrait (c.1939), by Wolf Willrich; oil painting, further details unavailable as, like much Nazi art, it was later destroyed.

One man's war

Some of the most memorable anti-Nazi works of art were made by German artist and pacifist John Heartfield. (He was actually born Helmut Herzfelde, but changed his name in 1916 to protest against German nationalism.) He developed a technique known as photomontage, combining sections of different photos. The results could be both savagely satirical and startlingly lifelike.

Adolf, the Superman shows Adolf Hitler making a speech. But an "X-ray" view of his insides shows he has been swallowing gold, and there is a Nazi swastika where his heart should be. Heartfield wanted to imply that Hitler was in the pay of rich industrialists and didn't really care about the people he claimed to represent. The Nazis retaliated by banning Heartfield's work and threatening to arrest him, and he was forced to leave Germany in 1933.

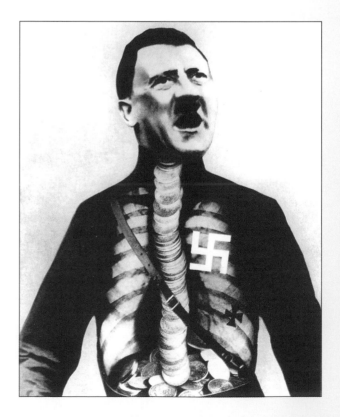

Adolf, the Superman: Swallows Gold and Spouts Junk (1932), by John Heartfield; photomontage, 14 x 10in. This image was designed as an anti-Hitler election poster.

The awful truth

Marc Chagall was a Russian Jew whose art tended to focus on mystical feelings rather than politics. But, in *White Crucifixion*, he set out to tell people the truth about Nazi Germany. The year he painted it, the Nazis attacked Jewish property and deported thousands of Jews or sent them to death camps. Chagall shows Jesus as a Jewish martyr, surrounded by scenes of mayhem and persecution. By combining all these different elements, Chagall linked the suffering of Jesus with the suffering of the Jews in his own time.

White Crucifixion (1938), by Marc Chagall; oil on canvas, 61 x 55in

Jesus is draped in a Jewish prayer shawl, and there is a Jewish candlestick at his feet. The lettering above his head calls him the "King of the Jews." Although Jesus was a Jew, he is rarely painted in this way.

On the left, a mob is advancing toward burning houses, waving red Communist flags. Topsy-turvy houses suggest a world turned upside down.

On the right, a German soldier is setting light to a synagogue, its contents ransacked and scattered on the ground.

Refugees flee left and right. One man clutches a sacred Jewish scroll, glancing back at flames billowing from another scroll. Beside him, a man wears a white placard like the ones German Jews were forced to wear, to show their religion.

Overhead, a group of biblical characters look on in tears.

Degenerate Art Exhibition

In their campaign against "degenerate" art, the Nazis confiscated over 17,000 artworks, including pieces by Munch, Picasso and Chagall, and used them to stage a "Degenerate Art Exhibition." This was designed to ridicule the art. The paintings were shown crowded together, with mocking labels. One Nazi critic called them "the crippled products of madness, impertinence and lack of talent." But ironically the exhibition proved very popular with the public, and attracted thousands of visitors each day. After the show closed, most of the art was sold to other countries to raise money for the Nazis. Anything left unsold was burned.

Aftermath

The Second World War saw many horrors, from ruthless fighting and the bombing of civilians to the systematic slaughter of millions in Nazi concentration camps. Shocked and disillusioned by events, a lot of people struggled to come to terms with what had happened, even years later, and this has been reflected in much of the art made since the war.

Human frailty

After the war, Alberto Giacometti began to draw and sculpt frail, stick-like people standing alone in space. *Man Pointing* is an early example. It shows a lone figure, as tall as a real man, but painfully thin. He is frozen in an unexplained gesture, pointing to something unseen. Such fragile, isolated figures expressed the anguish and uncertainty of the post-war period. Their thinness also evoked the suffering of the concentration camp victims, many of whom had starved to death.

Man Pointing (1947), by Swiss artist Alberto Giacometti; bronze, 70 x 37 x 20in

Horror show

Francis Bacon's *Three Studies for Figures at the Base of a Crucifixion* is filled with horror at the human condition. The three panels show deformed, tortured bodies, set against a blood-red background. The three-panel or "triptych" format was often used in Christian art and the title suggests the Christian theme of crucifixion.

You might expect it to refer to Jesus, whose death was meant to save mankind. But there is no sign of a savior in these pictures, and Bacon, who was an atheist, said he didn't intend the imagery to be Christian. According to him, the three figures are actually Furies – Greek goddesses of vengeance.

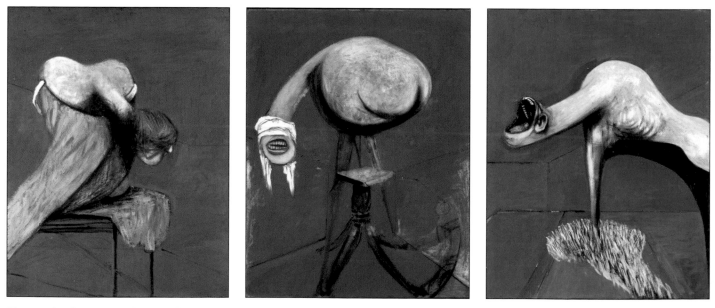

Three Studies for Figures at the Base of a Crucifixion (c.1944), by British painter Francis Bacon; oil on board, three panels, each 37 x 29in. Notice the intense red background color. It might suggest blood or fierce heat – or perhaps the fires of Hell?

Nameless Library (2000), by Rachel Whiteread; room-sized concrete cast. The red cylinders are candles left by visitors, to honor the dead.

In remembrance

In 2000, a new memorial designed by British artist Rachel Whiteread was unveiled in the Austrian capital, Vienna. Entitled *Nameless Library*, it commemorates the 65,000 Austrian Jews killed by the Nazis between 1938 and 1945. It was actually cast from real bookshelves, lined with thousands of books. Around the base are the names of the concentration camps to which Austria's Jewish population was deported.

Set in concrete, the library becomes a sealed chamber, with doors that can't be opened, full of books that can't be read – symbolizing the untold stories of all the victims' lives. It is a room turned inside out, a method which Whiteread said was meant to "invert people's perception of the world and to reveal the unexpected."

For links to websites where you can look at more paintings by Francis Bacon, or find out about another famous memorial, Maya Lin's *Wall*, which commemorates those who died in the Vietnam War, go to **www.usborne-quicklinks.com**

Public art

Memorials are one of the most common forms of public art. Until the first public art galleries and museums were built, around the beginning of the 19th century, public art – outdoor monuments and statues, and religious art in churches – was the only art that many people had ever seen. This kind of art has been a familiar part of our towns and cities for a long time. And it can still arouse strong feelings. *Nameless Library* is no exception.

When the *Library* was first planned, local residents complained its bunker-like design was ugly and out of keeping with the square where it was to be built. Then, construction was almost abandoned when workers uncovered the ruins of a medieval synagogue on the site. It had been burned in 1421, in an earlier wave of anti-Jewish attacks. Many Austrian Jews felt that the ruins would be a better memorial, but eventually a compromise was reached. The ruins were preserved beneath the modern monument, and today you can visit both.

NEW DIRECTIONS

During the 1950s and 60s, artists
continued to experiment and form
new avant-garde movements. But the
center of their activities changed.
Before the war, European cities such
as Paris had dominated the art scene.
After the war, the focus shifted to
New York, where many artists had
moved to escape the fighting.

Detail from *Mother and Child: Block Seat*
(1983-84), by Henry Moore. You can see the
whole sculpture on page 52.

New York, New York

In the 1940s-50s, a group of New York painters became world famous for a new kind of art called Abstract Expressionism. They weren't united by any particular style, but by the ambition and scale of their work. They created vast, abstract paintings meant to awe viewers and provoke deep emotional or spiritual responses. Their work had a huge impact, helping to turn New York into a major center for avant-garde art. And the city remained a focus for later movements such as Minimalism (see below right).

Number 1 (1948), by Jackson Pollock – probably the most famous Abstract Expressionist; oil and enamel on canvas, 68 x 104in

Action man

The Abstract Expressionists believed art should be a form of spontaneous personal expression. So they all developed their own, very individual ways of working. One artist, Jackson Pollock, specialized in densely textured paintings like *Number 1* – a canvas covered in a rich, tangled mass of splashes and streaks, with occasional splotches of color. Pollock made it by laying the canvas flat on the floor and splattering it with a brush. He also punctured paint cans and swung them over the surface with the paint pouring out. For thick, ridged lines, he squeezed oil paint directly from the tube. The drips, lines and splashes draw attention to the physical process of painting. And the boldness and density of the marks create an impression of restless energy and spontaneous rhythms. This method came to be known as Action Painting. For Pollock, it was so absorbing it was almost like a trance. He said, "When I am *in* my painting, I'm not aware of what I'm doing. It's only after a sort of 'get acquainted' period that I see what I have been about. I have no fears about making changes... because the painting has a life of its own."

Fields of color

Another New York artist, Mark Rothko, developed a style known as Color Field Painting, based on huge blocks of color. He painted with brushes and rags, giving the blocks such soft, hazy edges that they seem to float and shimmer, and almost come alive. His pictures are meant to absorb you in colors, shapes and textures. Some are like doorways or windows opening onto other worlds; others are like bars, locking you in.

Rothko hated the label "Abstract Expressionism," but he did admit that he wanted his art to communicate a particular feeling or state of mind. He said: "I'm interested only in expressing basic human emotions... The people who weep before my pictures are having the same religious experience I had when I painted them."

Right: *Number 8* (1952), by Mark Rothko; oil on canvas. The horizontal bands in this image create a sense of space, as if they were really sky and earth, separated by a yellow horizon.

Ursula's One and Two Picture 1/3 (1964), by Dan Flavin; fluorescent light fittings of various dimensions

Minimalism

Unlike the Abstract Expressionists, the Minimalists didn't want to make self-consciously "expressive" art. In fact, their ideas developed partly as a reaction against Abstract Expressionism. Their work was about reducing things to their simplest forms, exploring their physical qualities without trying to give them deeper meanings. For example, Frank Stella painted neat gray and black lines, while Carl Andre and Dan Flavin built plain, geometric shapes out of industrial materials such as bricks and lights.

Minimalism presents things just as they are, plain and unadorned. Flavin said of his work, "It is what it is and it ain't nothing else..." People have often criticized this approach for not being very "artistic," but it has had a great influence on modern art. But although Minimalism is a commonly used term, it was never an official movement and many so-called Minimalists have rejected the name.

Fierce arguments sprang up when the Tate Gallery in London bought a set of bricks named *Equivalent VIII*, by Carl Andre. Supporters said the work revealed the beauty of manufactured objects. But others said it was just a load of bricks.

Shaping up

In the 1930s and 40s, a new kind of sculpture emerged in Europe. At the forefront of the new style were two young British artists: Henry Moore and Barbara Hepworth. They created smooth, organic-looking sculptures, inspired by the natural world and their belief in being true to materials. This meant they tried to respond to the different qualities of wood or stone, or whatever they were working with at the time.

Natural rhythms

Henry Moore wanted to be a sculptor from the age of 11, when a teacher told him about the famous 16th-century sculptor Michelangelo. But he didn't want to imitate Michelangelo's detailed, lifelike style. Instead, Moore found his inspiration in the landscape, in the bodies of people and animals, and in ancient sculptures from around the world. Based on these, he created powerful, simplified figures like the one on the left. He wanted his works to be displayed outdoors, to help viewers see the connection between the sculptures and their surroundings.

Mother and Child: Block Seat is one of the last sculptures Moore ever made, and illustrates one of his favorite themes: maternity. It shows a woman sitting on a block-shaped seat, cradling her child. The sheltering, protective shape of the mother is enhanced by the sheltering trees which surround the work. Moore said he wanted his art to show "universal shapes to which everybody... can respond." The relationship between mother and child is one of the most basic, widespread human experiences, so it made an ideal universal subject. For Moore, it may also have been a reflection of his own creativity, since an artist gives life to art as a mother gives life to her child.

👁 For a link to a website where you can find out more about Henry Moore, see lots of his sculptures or explore 3-D panoramic views of his studio, go to **www.usborne-quicklinks.com**

Mother and Child: Block Seat (1983-84), by Henry Moore; bronze, height 96in. Notice how the mother's body curves protectively around her child.

Strings attached

Barbara Hepworth was friends with Henry Moore, and shared many of his ideas about art. But, while Moore achieved international recognition for his huge, bronze works – many of which are on display in public spaces in cities around the world – Hepworth tended to work on a smaller scale, using wood or stone. She spent much of her life by the sea, and often, her art seems to echo the shapes of waves, shells and sea-rounded pebbles.

Hepworth liked to follow the natural properties of her materials and let her sculptures evolve, rather than just carving them into set shapes. She was interested in the contrasts between different textures, and inner and outer surfaces. For example, she painted the inside of *Wave* a very pale blue, to contrast with the rich, polished wood of the sculpture itself. The pale hollow forms a delicate inner world, linked to its curving wooden shell by a series of taut threads.

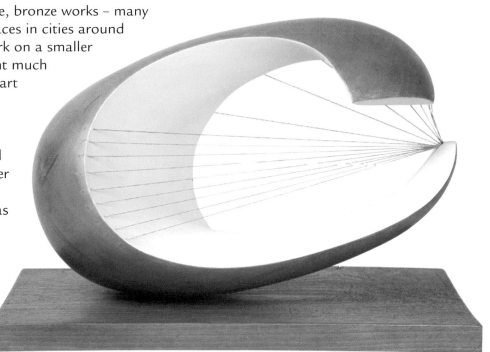

Wave (1943-44), by Barbara Hepworth; wood, paint and string, 12 x 18 x 8in. Does the curved shape remind you of the way a wave rolls and crashes onto a beach?

Distant echoes

Moore and Hepworth had a huge influence on modern sculpture, partly because of the way they worked with abstract shapes, but also because they made pieces that interact with the world around them. This is something that sculptors are still doing today.

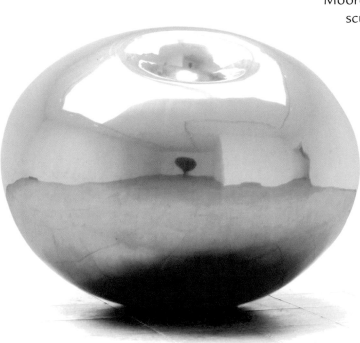

This dimpled steel sphere was created fairly recently by British sculptor Anish Kapoor. Its shiny, rounded shape makes it look a bit like an enormous drop of water. It is an interesting shape in itself. But its mirrored surface makes it even more interesting. When you look at the sculpture, you see yourself and your surroundings reflected in it. But the curved shape distorts appearances and makes everything look different – which may be why Kapoor called the piece *Turning the World Inside Out*.

Turning the World Inside Out (1995), by Anish Kapoor; stainless steel, 58 x 72 x 74in

On the streets

As the 20th century wore on, people's attitudes to cities changed. The early enthusiasm of groups like the Futurists was quelled by economic decline and the effects of two world wars. Increasingly, artists began to make art about urban decay or loneliness. Some artists built sculptures out of junk they found in the streets, while others found inspiration in urban graffiti.

For links to websites where you can see lots more street scenes by Edward Hopper, discover an unusual fountain designed by Jean Tinguely, or find out more about Jean-Michel Basquiat, go to **www.usborne-quicklinks.com**

Nighthawks (1942), by Edward Hopper; oil on canvas, 33 x 60in. Nighthawks are nocturnal birds – and so also a nickname for people who do things at night. Notice the strong contrasts between light and dark. They create a moody, almost cinematic effect, like the lighting used in *film noir* – movies about urban crime and corruption popular in the 1930s-40s. The picture is shaped like a movie screen, too.

Lonely nights

American artist Edward Hopper became known for painting atmospheric scenes of urban life – empty streets, lonely buildings and roads going nowhere. *Nighthawks* shows a late-night diner overlooking a deserted street corner. According to Hopper, the picture was based on a real restaurant in New York. But there is nothing to identify it – the picture could be set in any one of hundreds of U.S. cities. Hopper claimed he didn't set out to paint symbols of isolation or emptiness. But he did admit that in this painting, "unconsciously, probably, I was painting the loneliness of a large city."

Much of the effect comes from the way Hopper painted light. The harsh glare in the diner is probably due to fluorescent lights, which began to be used in the 1930s-40s. The light spills out onto the street, creating an eerie glow on the pavement and leaving deep, menacing shadows in the corners. It makes the brightly lit interior seem like a refuge. But there is no sign of an entrance, just an unbroken wall of glass separating the viewer from the people inside. And those people seem to be cut off from each other, too. They aren't talking to one another, just sitting there absorbed in their own thoughts.

Urban junk

Swiss sculptor Jean Tinguely made "Kinetic" (meaning "moving") sculptures out of urban junk. Their movements were generally chaotic and sometimes destructive. So perhaps Tinguely meant to criticize the power of machines – unlike the Futurists, who celebrated them. One of his most famous constructions, entitled *Homage to New York*, self-destructed in 1960, outside the Museum of Modern Art in New York. It included a painting machine, a device which billowed out clouds of white smoke, and a piano that played while going up in flames.

Homage to New York ran for 27 minutes, creating a huge racket, until it destroyed itself.

Surviving fragment of *Homage to New York* (1960), by Jean Tinguely. The original sculpture was 26ft high. It was built out of bottles, bicycle and buggy wheels, a bathtub, a balloon, a bell, a car horn, a radio, playing cards, fire extinguishers, scraps of the U.S. flag, a hammer and a saw – all powered by 15 engines.

Graffiti art

The art of New York painter Jean-Michel Basquiat is often related to graffiti, although he hated being labeled as a "graffiti artist." And the idea of graffiti as "art" is itself controversial, since it is illegal to deface other people's property. But Basquiat began his career doing just that, scrawling pictures and slogans signed "SAMO" on walls around New York. Even after Basquiat began painting on canvases instead of walls, his pictures still had many graffiti-like qualities. They are built up out of overlapping layers and fragments, using simple, spiky shapes, often with scrawled words. Some were done on canvas stretched over frames made from junk found in the streets. The images are vivid and expressive, based on Basquiat's feelings and experiences as a young Black man growing up in the U.S. Some of them celebrate Black American history or street culture. But others seem to be about anger or violence.

Gas Truck (1985), by Hispanic-African-American artist Jean-Michel Basquiat; acrylic and oil on canvas, 50 x 165in

Being popular

The post-war era saw a huge boom in mass-produced goods and mass entertainment. This gave rise to a new popular – or "pop" – culture. Many artists responded by borrowing elements of pop culture to create something now known as Pop art. This emerged in England but soon spread to New York, and many of the most famous Pop artists were American.

Pop rebellion

People often distinguish "high culture," such as paintings – which are expensive and often seen only by a small elite – from pop culture, which is available to everybody. But Pop art defied this distinction, by taking images from magazines, television and other mass media, and by copying commercial mass-production techniques. The Pop artists were also rebelling against the success of Abstract Expressionism, which they thought was too pretentious and inward-looking.

Whaam! (1963), by Roy Lichtenstein; acrylic on canvas, 68 x 160in. This painting imitates the style of printed comic books. If you look closely, you can see dots like the ones produced by some printing presses. What you can't see is the scale – in real life, this picture covers a whole wall.

Just what is it...?

This 1956 collage by British artist Richard Hamilton is sometimes called the first Pop picture. It shows a modern-looking room with a photograph of the moon looming overhead – perhaps a reference to the race between the U.S. and the U.S.S.R. to put a man on the moon. On the left, a body-builder grasps a huge red lollipop labeled "POP." On the right, a woman poses provocatively beneath a poster celebrating romance. Together, they form a kind of "ideal" couple – or a parody of one. They are surrounded by assorted consumer items, including an extendable vacuum cleaner, a reel-to-reel tape recorder and a can of ham, cut from magazines and catalogs. It is a ridiculous combination, making a mockery of advertising and the picture-perfect life it tries to sell us.

Just What Is It That Makes Today's Homes So Different, So Appealing? (1956), by Richard Hamilton; collage, 10 x 10in. Even the title of this picture parodies the language of adverts.

Mass-produced art

Roy Lichtenstein and Andy Warhol were among the best-known American Pop artists. Lichtenstein painted huge comic-book pictures such as *Whaam!* Was he suggesting that comics deserve to be considered "art," or trying to make us take a critical look at comic-book values? According to him, comics "express violent emotion in a completely mechanical and removed style." He imitated them so closely, he even copied the colored dots used in cheap printing.

Warhol went a step further, making prints of everything from soup cans to movie stars. (You can see an example on pages 60-61.) For him, art was no longer about creating something unique. He even named his studio "The Factory," comparing his work to mass production.

Questions of taste

Pop art was very successful very quickly, perhaps because people found it amusing and easy to understand. Hamilton ironically defined it as: "Popular (designed for a mass audience), Transient (short term solution), Expendable (easily forgotten), Low cost, Mass-produced, Young (aimed at youth), Witty, Sexy, Gimmicky, Glamorous, Big business." Compared to the serious abstract works artists had done in the 1950s, Pop seemed light-hearted and fun. And the commercial images and techniques it imitated were designed to have a broad appeal. But not everyone liked it. Some critics referred to Pop art as "New Vulgarism," because they felt Pop artists had lost sight of art's more serious goals.

Staying popular

Pop has had a lasting influence, even today, in the work of artists like Jeff Koons. Like the Pop artists, he turns everyday objects into art. For example, he took a rabbit-shaped balloon – deliberately selecting a trashy or "kitsch" object – and made it into a polished steel sculpture. It might look amusing, but do you think it was meant to have a serious message? Perhaps Koons meant to celebrate consumer culture, or comment on the throwaway nature of society, by making a throwaway item such as a balloon into something more permanent.

Rabbit (1986), by Jeff Koons; cast stainless steel, 41 x 19 x 12in. Koons has made several works based on novelty balloons like this.

A Bigger Splash

British artist David Hockney moved to California in the 1960s, drawn by the sunny Californian climate and relaxed way of life. It inspired him to create many colorful, idealized paintings of life there. *A Bigger Splash* captures the moment as a diver enters a cool, blue pool beneath a luminous turquoise sky.

Title: *A Bigger Splash*
Date: 1967
Artist: David Hockney
Materials: acrylic on canvas
Size: 96 x 96in

Real and imagined

Although this scene looks very realistic, Hockney actually made it up. He based the pool on a photograph he had seen in a book about swimming pools. The background, with its low-slung, 1960s-style house, he took from a drawing he had done of buildings in California.

The clear horizontal lines of the house and pool contrast strongly with the diagonal diving board and the spindly, vertical palm trees. It is a curiously empty picture – the only sign of life is the splash itself. The house windows reflect other buildings, suggesting this is an urban scene. But, oddly – or perhaps because this is an imaginary picture – there are no buildings visible behind the house, giving the impression of vast open space beyond.

Plastic paint

The bold colors stress the intensity of the Californian sunlight. The yellow diving board stands out dramatically against the cool blue of the water, and the pink house contrasts with the bright blue sky. Hockney had recently begun to use acrylic paints instead of traditional oils. Acrylic paints are based on plastics and were only invented in the 1950s. They give very strong colors and dry much faster than oils, so they were good for the sunny colors and sharp outlines of Hockney's painting.

Hockney was always ready to experiment with new techniques, even making art out of fax machine print-outs.

Rolled and brushed

Hockney emphasized the way the splash breaks the stillness of the pool by the way he applied his paints. He did the main blocks of color first, using rollers to get a very smooth surface. Then he painted in the details with brushes. For the splash itself, he used deliberately rough, textured brushstrokes, to contrast with the smooth blue water and the flat surfaces in the background.

Hockney chose to leave a border of unpainted canvas around the scene, to frame it. (The canvas is the background color of these pages.)

Frozen moments

Although the splash would have lasted only moments, this painting took Hockney about two weeks to finish. He compared this with the way a photograph "freezes" a moment, saying: "I realize that a splash could never be seen this way in real life, it happens too quickly. And I was amused by this, so I painted it in a very, very slow way."

Everyday pop

Hockney's work became famous at about the same time as Pop art. People often associate him with that movement, although he has always rejected the label. But he was painting ordinary, everyday things in a straightforward way – something many Pop artists were doing too.

👁 For a link to a website where you can take an online tour of one of the biggest collections of Hockney's work, go to **www.usborne-quicklinks.com**

Famous faces

Pop art drew heavily on pop culture, so it is not surprising that it often featured famous faces from movies and pop music. But the relationship between artists and celebrities got even closer, with some movie and pop stars commissioning or making art, and some artists becoming famous in their own right.

Famous for 15 minutes

Andy Warhol was fascinated by fame. He held celebrity parties in his studio and made sure his own image, complete with artificial white wig, became well known. Much of his art dealt with fame, too. He made colorful prints of movie stars like Marilyn Monroe and Liz Taylor. *Elvis I & II* shows the singer Elvis Presley, posing with a gun for a movie called *Flaming Star*, repeated four times. The mechanical repetition makes it impersonal, reminding you that this is a screen image, not a personal portrait. And, as you look across the canvas, the image blurs and fades into black and white. Perhaps this was about the short-lived nature of fame? Warhol once predicted fame would become briefer and briefer. He said, "In the future everyone will be world-famous for 15 minutes."

Elvis I & II (1964), by Andy Warhol; synthetic polymer paint, aluminum paint and silkscreen ink on canvas, two panels, each 82 x 82in – just over lifesize. Notice how each Elvis is slightly different from the others. Though they are printed, they are not exact copies. How they look depends partly on chance.

Album cover: *Sgt. Pepper's Lonely Hearts Club Band* (1967), by Peter Blake; photograph, 12 x 12in

Art and commerce

Although Pop art was originally inspired by commercial art, it soon became a two-way relationship, with many Pop artists also working in advertising or design. For example, Warhol's art grew out of his experience of drawing advertisements and designing shop windows. As the pop music industry boomed, some artists began to design record covers. This led to one of the most famous pieces of commercial Pop art – the cover for The Beatles' album, *Sgt. Pepper's Lonely Hearts Club Band* (1967). Its distinctive collage-style look was created by British artist Peter Blake. It shows the band among a crowd of lifesize cardboard cutouts and models. The colorful figures in the middle are the real Beatles; they appear again as wax models on the left, this time in dark suits. The other figures are well-known actors, singers, artists, writers, spiritual leaders and sports stars, meant to represent the band's ideal audience.

Celebrity art

As the world today seems obsessed with fame, it is perhaps only natural that art reflects this. Now, art and celebrity appear closer than ever. Stars such as the singer Madonna are known as art collectors, while others, such as former Beatle Paul McCartney, have turned to painting. In fact, many musicians, including David Bowie and the pop group Blur, began their careers at art school. The idea of the celebrity-artist cultivated by Warhol continues with artists like Damien Hirst, who is often in the news. Artists still work with pop music – Blake recently did a cover for singer Robbie Williams. And artists continue to explore the nature of fame, too. For example, Michael Jackson has featured in paintings by Gary Hume. And Sam Taylor-Wood (see page 70) filmed pop star Kylie Minogue miming naked to opera to create a work entitled *The Misfit*.

👁 For links to websites where you can read about the making of the *Sgt. Pepper* album cover and discover who all the people in the crowd are, or view lots more prints by Andy Warhol, go to **www.usborne-quicklinks.com**

Faces in the crowd

Among the artists sampling the pop culture of today is Black British painter Chris Ofili. He uses pictures from magazines, along with brightly colored pins and deliberately rough-looking lumps of elephant dung, to create works like *Afrodizzia*. This features hundreds of black faces, including famous musicians James Brown, Louis Armstrong and Michael Jackson, set in a swirling mass of color. The picture captures the energy and excitement of their music, as well as paying tribute to black musical traditions.

Ofili compared painting to writing a song, saying, "you want to get the right rhythm and base line." He builds up his pictures in layers, borrowing bits of other images, rather like music sampling. His unusual techniques were also inspired by his sense of his African heritage. The bead-like dots of paint were influenced by African cave paintings. He started using elephant dung after bringing some back from Africa – though he now gets supplies from London Zoo.

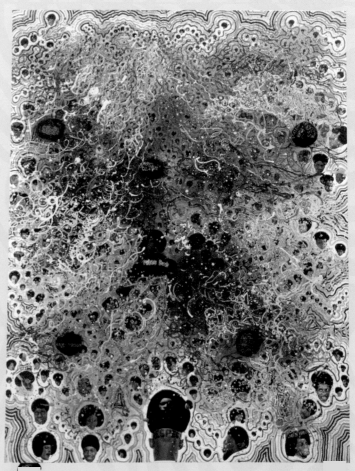

Afrodizzia (1996), by Chris Ofili; acrylic, oil, resin, paper collage, glitter, map pins and elephant dung on canvas, 96 x 72in. This painting rests on elephant-dung feet.

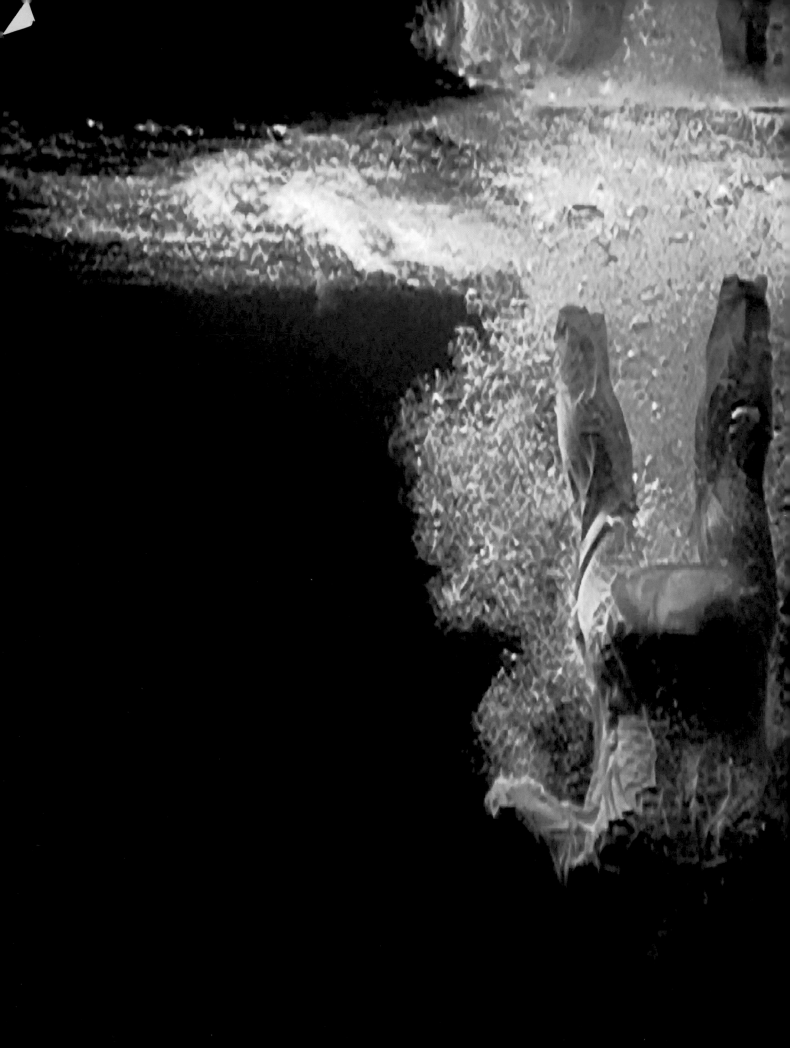

ANYTHING GOES

Art can mean almost anything nowadays, with artists using everything from traditional oil paints to the latest medical imaging technology. Artists have taken art outside galleries too, creating works outdoors and in some startlingly unexpected places and ways.

Detail of *Departing Angel* from *Five Angels for the Millennium* (2001), by Bill Viola. You can find out more about this video and sound installation on page 71.

Beyond the frame

To many artists in the 1960s-70s, traditional painting and sculpture felt too limited. They wanted to make art that would stretch the definition of what "art" really was – and perhaps change people's ideas about the world, too. So they began to create a different kind of art, by recording ideas, staging performances or building things. These works had no frame to keep them separate from their audience, so they couldn't be looked at in a traditional way.

> 👁 For a link to a website where you can read about a Conceptual work entitled *Pharmacy* by Damien Hirst, and see photographs showing how it changed as it was installed in different art galleries around the world, go to **www.usborne-quicklinks.com**

What's the big idea?

The term "Conceptual art" began to be used in the 1960s. It describes art where the concept or idea behind the work is more important than anything the artist actually makes. In fact, there is often no artwork at all, only written notes or photographs explaining the artist's idea. For example, how many chairs do you see on the right? There is only one actual chair – but there is also a photograph of it and the text of a dictionary entry for "chair." So, as the title says, there are both "One and Three Chairs." In this way, the piece explores the nature of reality and how it can be represented in pictures or words.

One and Three Chairs (1965), by Joseph Kosuth; photograph of a chair, wooden chair and dictionary entry for "chair"

Acting up

Some of Yves Klein's art was created by live models. He called them "living brushes."

Performance art – also sometimes known as "Happenings" – was designed to blur the boundaries between art, theater and real life. In a series of performances known as *Anthropometries*, Yves Klein got nude models to smear themselves with paint and roll on paper in front of an audience, accompanied by live music. The finished paintings were mounted and framed, but the process of creating them was considered as important as the end result.

Explaining away

In a 1965 Happening, *How to explain paintings to a dead hare*, Joseph Beuys covered his head with honey and gold leaf, tied a length of iron to one foot, and went around a Düsseldorf gallery with a dead hare, explaining the pictures on display. Although Beuys must have looked very odd, he wouldn't have minded. To him, the piece was "about the problems of thought [and] consciousness." To act it out, he had to express his thoughts. But, because the hare could not listen or understand, Beuys also showed how we may fail to communicate our ideas to others.

Beuys described his work as "anti-art," because he wanted to reject art's traditional values and uses. He didn't want to make beautiful things. Instead, he believed that art could change society – and that "Everyone is an artist."

Installing art

An installation is the name given to a 3-D work that takes over a whole room or field or other space, and creates a new environment of its own. Probably the biggest example is Robert Rauschenberg's ¼ *Mile or 2 Furlong Piece*. This includes hundreds of elements, from street signs and stacks of books and boxes, to collages and prints, and even sounds such as traffic or a baby crying. It is about trying to show the structure within seemingly random arrangements – what Rauschenberg called "Random Order."

¼ *Mile or 2 Furlong Piece* (1981-present), by Robert Rauschenberg; mixed media, variable dimensions. Rauschenberg is still adding to this. When it's finished, he wants it to stretch the full length of its title. Its progress records the artist's life and art as it has developed over time.

Cell (Hands and Mirror) (1995), by Louise Bourgeois; marble, painted metal and mirror, 63 x 48 x 45in

In the cells

French-American sculptor Louise Bourgeois made a series of installations that she called "cells." As the name suggests, they are small, enclosed spaces, which viewers peer into through shuttered windows or half-open doors, creating an uneasy, claustrophobic feeling. The cell on the left contains a shaving mirror and a pair of hands on a block of stone, the fingers knotted together as if in pain. According to Bourgeois, the cells represent different types of pain: "the physical, the emotional and the psychological, and the mental and intellectual." Some of her cells use broken glass and menacing industrial machines to suggest suffering. Perhaps here, the pain is meant to be the lack of privacy – the mirror and open shutters invite us to look at the hands from every angle. The shape of the cell is important too. The walls form a circle, so there is no beginning or end point – just a continuous cycle.

Cold Dark Matter

The installation *Cold Dark Matter*, by British artist Cornelia Parker, is a mass of debris suspended on invisible wires in a darkened room. A single light bulb shines in the middle, so all the bits and pieces cast eerie shadows on the walls. They are actually the charred remains of a garden shed packed with old junk and plastic explosive, and blown up by the British Army.

Title: *Cold Dark Matter: An Exploded View*
Artist: Cornelia Parker   Date: 1991
Size: approx. 157 x 197 x 197in
Materials: a garden shed and contents blown up for the artist by the British army, the fragments suspended around a light bulb

What is the matter?

The splintered pieces of wood around the outside are the fragments of the shed itself. Hanging between them is an odd assortment of junk, including old books, letters, shoes, toys, garden tools, bicycle parts and a twisted bucket. "I like to take man-made objects and push them... so that they become something else," explained Parker. Here, she has taken ordinary, everyday items discarded by other people and turned them into art.

The title works on several levels. Sheds are often cold, dark places. "Cold dark matter" is also a term from astronomy. According to Parker, it is "the material within the universe that we cannot see and we cannot quantify. We know it exists but we can't measure it." So the title suggests a link with science and outer space. Many scientists believe the universe was formed by a huge explosion known as the "Big Bang." Perhaps this installation is meant to be a kind of small-scale version of that cosmic event?

👁 For a link to a website where you can see more works by Parker, including one named *Mass (Colder Darker Matter)*, go to **www.usborne-quicklinks.com**

Right: *Breathless*
(2001), by Cornelia
Parker; brass musical
instruments flattened and
suspended, seen against a round ceiling

The art of destruction

Parker makes art in very unconventional ways. As well as blowing
things up, she has run over coins with a train and crushed
pieces of silver – plates, candlesticks, spoons, boxes and
trophies – with a steamroller. For *Breathless,* she created an
arrangement of squashed brass instruments. Although
their shapes are instantly recognizable, the flattened
instruments really did become "breathless" and
unplayable – to the anger of some musicians.

For one installation, Parker steamrollered
more than 1,000 silver objects and
arranged them into 30 neat, round piles.
She called it *30 Pieces of Silver,* referring to
the Bible story about Judas, who betrayed
Jesus for 30 pieces of silver.

Parker described what she does to her objects as "cartoon deaths" – and
there is something comic about the way she destroys them. But there is
also something touching about the way she selects broken, discarded
items and resurrects them through art. But she avoids pinning down the
meaning of her work, saying, "All I try to do... is to make something that
makes the hairs on the back of my neck stand up, and then I hope that it
might do that for someone else."

The great outdoors

A lot of modern art takes art out of galleries and into places that you wouldn't normally think of – from remote country landscapes to busy urban environments. Some artists have chosen to do this because they are trying to make people aware of environmental issues. Others want to make art that cannot be bought and sold, and to make people look at the world in new ways.

> 👁 For links to websites where you can see many examples of Land and Environmental art, go to **www.usborne-quicklinks.com**

Mud Hand Circles (1989), by Richard Long; circles of mud handprints, about 126in across. Long made this painting on a wall in Jesus College, Cambridge, using mud he brought back from the River Avon.

Working the land

Landscapes have always been a traditional subject for paintings. But in the 1960s and 70s, some artists began to work directly with the land, making art out in the open and then documenting it. They used natural materials and allowed changes in the weather and light to add to the result. This approach is known as Land art, or Earthworks. It can range from huge mounds made with bulldozers to something as small and short-lived as a line of crushed grass.

British artist Richard Long became known for making Land art based on walks in wild, remote places, which he records with maps, poems and photos. On some walks, he builds simple arrangements of stones or driftwood. Sometimes, he collects natural materials to make similar pieces back in the gallery. *Mud Hand Circles* is one example. Like much of Long's work, it explores the relationship between people – represented by the handprints – and nature. With large-scale Earthworks, probably the best-known examples are American. One artist, Robert Smithson, built a huge spiral jetty in the Great Salt Lake, Utah, using vast quantities of rock and earth.

U.S. artist Walter De Maria covered an enormous field with a grid of steel poles designed to attract lightning.

Snow and ice

British artist Andy Goldsworthy makes art inspired by specific landscapes, from English woodland to the Arctic wastes. He gathers natural materials, such as leaves and feathers, and arranges them in simple shapes. He has even worked with snow and ice, creating giant snowballs and delicate sculptures such as *Icicle Star*. His art is designed to interact with its setting and often doesn't last long, reflecting the changes that occur in nature. Like Long, he is interested in exploring the relationship between people and the world around them.

Icicle Star (1987), by Andy Goldsworthy. This was made of icicles stuck together with frozen water. But it has long since melted and now exists only in photographs.

All wrapped up

For two weeks in 1995, the *Reichstag*, the German parliament building in Berlin, was swathed in silvery fabric held in place by blue ropes. This project was planned by two artists who call themselves Christo and Jeanne-Claude. They describe their work as Environmental art (not Land art) because they do it in many different places, not just out in the wild.

Wrapped Reichstag, Berlin (1971-95), by Christo and Jeanne-Claude. This required special permission from the German government, and a huge team of workers and professional climbers.

Under cover

The fabric transformed the Reichstag, hiding its usual appearance but revealing its basic shape. The project also had a political meaning. As the seat of the German parliament, the building is also a symbol of German democracy. So for many people *Wrapped Reichstag* was a reminder of the difficult struggle Germany had to achieve democracy.

Religious visions

Although many artists now use materials and techniques that weren't available in the past, their art often deals with the same issues. Since about the 5th century, Christianity has been one of the main subjects of western art – a lot of art was made to tell Bible stories or provide a focus for prayer. For a time, modern art pushed religion to the margins. But, over the past decade, it has re-emerged as a major theme.

Pieta (2001), by Sam Taylor-Wood; 35mm film/DVD, duration: 1 minute 57 seconds. The film runs in a loop, with no sound and almost no movement. The pose of the two figures in the film was inspired by a marble sculpture made five centuries earlier, by famous Italian artist Michelangelo Buonarroti.

Moving pictures

Sam Taylor-Wood's *Pieta* takes an old Christian theme and gives it a modern twist by turning it into a film. *Pieta* is Italian for "pity." In art, it usually means a painting or statue of the Virgin Mary with the body of her dead son, Jesus. Taylor-Wood's film shows a woman cradling a man's lifeless body. It is an awkward pose – the woman's muscles strain to take the weight, and the man's arm dangles stiffly. But the result is a striking image of sadness and dignity in the face of death. Taylor-Wood assumes the role of Mary, and actor Robert Downey Jr. takes the part of Jesus. This has led some critics to link the film's concern with suffering to the artist's own fight against cancer, and Downey's struggle with addiction.

Small angel

Ron Mueck is known for creating incredibly lifelike figures – in fact, he started out making models for television and movies. His work is painstakingly crafted, down to each individual hair. The results are so convincing, they are often dubbed "hyperreal." But they are also unreal, because Mueck plays with sizes in startling ways. For example, *Angel* is a tiny figure slumped on a stool and dwarfed by his own wings, which seem to weigh heavily on his shoulders. Despite his name, he looks far from angelic. His face is set in a sulky scowl, and his head is propped sadly in his hands. Being good, this sculpture seems to suggest, isn't necessarily fun.

Angel (1997), by Australian artist Ron Mueck; silicon rubber and mixed media, 43 x 34 x 32in. The body was modeled in clay before being cast out of rubber. The wings are made of white goose feathers.

Man to man

When British artist Mark Wallinger was asked to do a new artwork for an empty plinth in London's Trafalgar Square, he decided to make a statue of Jesus. He named it *Ecce Homo*, which is Latin for "Behold the man." According to the Bible, this is what was said as Jesus was shown to the crowd just before his crucifixion. So it was appropriate for this work to be displayed in a busy city square. The statue shows Jesus as he would have looked at that moment, wearing a loin-cloth and a crown of thorns, with his hands tied behind his back.

Wallinger modeled the statue on a real man. It looked tiny on the plinth, which was designed for a much grander monument. But Wallinger didn't want to make his statue any larger than life. He said his aim was to show Jesus "as an ordinary human being." But he cast the statue out of pale white marble resin, which gives it a ghostly effect. So it seems both lifelike and other-worldly at the same time.

Ecce Homo (1999), by Mark Wallinger; marble resin, lifesize. This photograph shows the statue as it appeared in Trafalgar Square, the first in a series of temporary displays on the plinth.

For a link to a website where you can see other artworks which have been displayed on Trafalgar Square's empty plinth, go to **www.usborne-quicklinks.com**

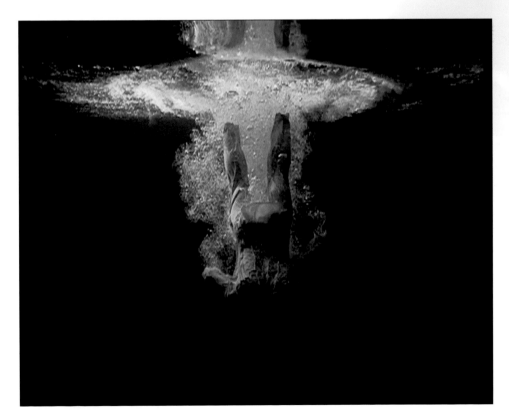

Millennium angels

American artist Bill Viola uses video to explore spirituality and basic life experiences such as birth and death. *Five Angels for the Millennium* is a set of five simultaneous video projections. They show an underwater world which is sometimes sky blue, sometimes fiery red – the colors of Heaven and Hell. Periodically, a human figure appears in a burst of noise and light, rising up out of the water or plunging down into it. But the movement is slowed down, so it seems strange and mystical, like the arrival or departure of an angel.

Departing Angel from *Five Angels for the Millennium* (2001), by Bill Viola; video and sound installation

Model relationships

For some artists and critics, especially feminists who are concerned with women's rights, the role of women in art has been a troubled and neglected political issue.

In the past, a lot of art was made by men for men, and many women felt it failed to represent their point of view. But recently, women artists have set out to challenge this.

Left: *Dancing Ostriches from Walt Disney's Fantasia* (1995), by Portuguese-born artist Paula Rego; pastel on paper mounted on aluminum, 59 x 59in. This picture was inspired by cartoon ostriches similar to the ones below.

When Rego was asked to create art based on movies, she did a series of pastel drawings inspired by Disney cartoons. The women on the left are her version of the dancing ostriches in *Fantasia*.

Telling stories

Paula Rego often creates pictures based on stories, especially ones with strong female characters. Here, she drew three women in ballet costumes and poses taken from Walt Disney's *Fantasia*. Disney's artists sketched real dancers, and then turned them into ostriches. Rego reversed this and turned the birds back into real women. She said, "I always want to turn things on their heads, to upset the established order."

Surprisingly, though, the women in Rego's drawing aren't actually dancing. Two are propped on cushions, while the third hitches up her skirt. Despite their ribbons and tutus, they don't look much like ballerinas – their bodies are too heavy and middle-aged. But the picture isn't really about ballet. It's about the women themselves, and the conflict between their dreams and their aging bodies.

Packing a punch

American artist Barbara Kruger began her career designing magazines and often uses magazine pictures in her art, combined with short, punchy phrases. The effect is meant to challenge people's ideas about power and identity. She says she works with pictures and words because they have "the ability to determine who we are."

Your Gaze Hits the Side of My Face is a stark, black and white photo of a woman's head, sculpted in a fairly traditional-looking style. The woman's face is turned modestly away. But the words on the left make it seem as if she is speaking out, accusing viewers of not seeing below the surface/side of her face. Kruger wanted to illustrate the feminist belief that traditional art shows women only as objects to be looked at, rather than as the people doing the looking.

Untitled (Your Gaze Hits the Side of My Face) (1981), by Barbara Kruger; lithograph, 55 x 41in. Notice how Kruger uses slogan-like text and stylish photography to create something which resembles an advertisement.

Guerilla tactics

There has been a lot of feminist criticism of the art of the past, especially of female nudes such as *Odalisque* by 19th-century French artist Ingres. It is a beautiful painting, but the politics behind it may be less attractive. An "odalisque" was a female slave, so this woman is being shown in a powerless, submissive role. She would have been meant to appeal to male viewers. Nearly two centuries later, Ingres' painting appeared in a very different way, on a poster designed by the "Guerilla Girls" – an anonymous group of women artists who campaign on political issues. The poster compared the number of female nudes with the number of works by women artists in the prestigious Metropolitan Museum in New York. The Guerilla Girls wanted to draw attention to what they saw as an unfair, if unconscious, bias in the art world, where the majority of critics and curators are men.

👁 For links to websites where you can find out more about the artists on these pages, go to **www.usborne-quicklinks.com**

Odalisque (1814), by Jean-Auguste-Dominique Ingres; oil on canvas, 36 x 64in. This painting hangs in the Louvre Museum in Paris.

Do women... (1989), by the Guerilla Girls; billboard poster. This was created for the Public Art Fund in New York – who refused to display it.

Taking pictures

Many people wonder if photography is really art – partly because it depends on chemical processes rather than skill with a paintbrush. But photographs still have to be composed and printed. They aren't always about recording how things look, either. The artists here used photographs to create imaginary characters and experiment with the whole idea of image-making.

> 👁 For links to websites where you can see more of Cindy Sherman's *Untitled Film Stills* or another photomontage by David Hockney, go to **www.usborne-quicklinks.com**

Moving pictures

In the late 1970s and early 80s, American artist Cindy Sherman made a series of photographs called *Untitled Film Stills*. They weren't really taken from films, but are lit and framed in a cinematic way. Sherman said they were inspired by movie publicity shots.

Sherman herself appears in each photograph, dressed up like a Hollywood actress playing a clichéd role, such as a runaway lover or a young housewife. Many people think the images are meant to draw attention to film stereotypes about women. But, unlike real film stills, there are no fixed stories behind these pictures, so it is up to the viewer to decide how to interpret them.

Untitled Film Still #48 (1979), by Cindy Sherman; photograph on paper, 30 x 40in

Happy days

Like Sherman, British artists Gilbert and George made themselves the subjects of their art. In 1970, they began to call themselves "living sculptures." Then they started taking pictures of themselves. They became known for creating huge, bright, grid-like arrangements of photos, which look rather like modern stained glass windows.

Happy is from a series entitled "Modern Fears," made at the start of the 1980s. The series dealt with the artists' everyday life, including their fears, fantasies and moods. Here, they are making grotesque faces – despite the title, they seem anything but happy. The yellow face appears worried or scared, and the red one looks like a creature from a horror movie. The lighting adds to the horror-movie effect – both faces are lit from below, casting sinister shadows. But many people enjoy being scared by horror movies, so perhaps the picture is meant to make viewers happy by giving them a similar thrill?

Happy (1980), by Gilbert and George; photographs on paper, 95 x 79in

My Mother, Los Angeles, Dec. 1982 (1982), by David Hockney; photographic collage, 53 x 39in

Notice the jumps in colors and angles where one photo overlaps the next. The carpet varies from mustard to reddish-brown or beige, showing how much the appearance of something can vary in different photographs.

Multiple views

David Hockney has made large photographic collages, which he dubbed "multiples," made up of dozens or even hundreds of individual photos. He combined the photos in a deliberately disjointed way, sometimes overlapping, sometimes with gaps – like this portrait of his mother. Each photograph offers a slightly different glimpse of the scene, so there are strange jumps and distortions, and abrupt changes of color. Hockney linked this technique to Cubism.

Like a Cubist painting, it shows everything from multiple viewpoints, so you see an array of separate details, rather than a unified whole. It also shows just how incomplete each individual photograph really is. But Hockney overcame this limitation by combining multiple views. For example, in the collage above, you can see both the artist's feet at the bottom and the ceiling at the top – a far wider view than you could get in a single shot.

Me, myself and I

Self portraits have been popular with artists for at least 500 years, ever since good mirrors became available. But, now photographic portraits are so widespread, artists are no longer as concerned with capturing a likeness. Some of them have chosen to explore very unusual techniques instead.

For a link to a website where you can see another self portrait by Chuck Close and find out more about his painting methods, go to **www.usborne-quicklinks.com**

Flesh and blood

Marc Quinn has made a lot of sculptures based on his own body. Probably the best known is *Self* – a model of his head made from his own blood. It took Quinn five months to have enough blood extracted. The blood was then poured into a mold and frozen. Its reddish color gives the face an unexpected, almost sinister look. It makes the head seem both familiar and strange, like Quinn's view of his "self." "The self is what one knows best and least at the same time," he said. The features look frost-bitten, creating a frightening sense of decay. But the calm expression gives the head a peaceful look. The eyes are shut as if in death, like a traditional death mask – a cast of a dead person's face taken to preserve his or her memory. The fragility of the sculpture (it has to be kept in a refrigerated case) also adds to its meaning, by reminding you just how fragile life is.

Self (1991), by Marc Quinn; blood, stainless steel, perspex and refrigeration equipment, case 82 x 25 x 25in. This artwork contains almost as much blood as an average human body.

Photorealistic

American artist Chuck Close specializes in huge portraits, done in a detailed, almost photographic style known as Photorealism. Close actually starts by projecting a photograph onto a gridded canvas. Then he fills in the grid, square by square. To begin with, he used an airbrush to get a flat, even finish. But, in 1988, a blood clot in his neck left him badly paralyzed. This made him develop a new, more expressive technique using brushes strapped to his wrists.

The self portrait on the left was done with brushes. Although it looks very realistic, if you stand very close to it, it dissolves into a near-abstract pattern of shapes and colors. Close described his pictures as "paintings first and portraits second." They are designed to challenge our assumption that photos are "real."

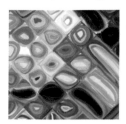

Self Portrait (1997) by Chuck Close; oil on canvas, 102 x 84in. The enlarged detail on the right shows Close's colorful, looping brushstrokes.

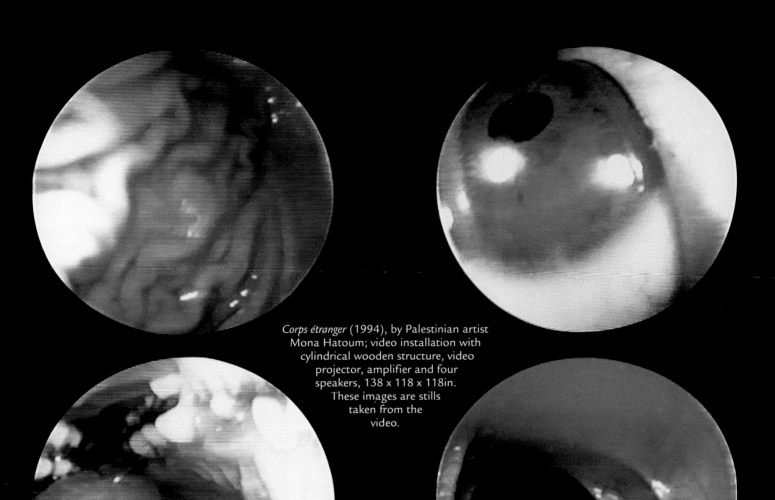

Corps étranger (1994), by Palestinian artist Mona Hatoum; video installation with cylindrical wooden structure, video projector, amplifier and four speakers, 138 x 118 x 118in. These images are stills taken from the video.

Inner self

Much of Mona Hatoum's art is about bodies, both her own and that of the viewer. *Corps étranger* is a film of a journey through her body, projected onto the floor of a tall white cylinder, which you enter through a narrow doorway. The filming itself was done by a surgeon using a miniature fiber optic camera. The film begins by showing the outside of Hatoum's body in extreme close-up, revealing tiny details such as the pores in her skin or the veins in her eyes. Then the camera plunges right inside her body, down her throat and into moist, pulsating tunnels, accompanied by the sound of her breathing and heartbeats.

The film magnifies everything to an impossible size, revealing things you couldn't normally see. It makes bodies seem strange, both attractive and repulsive at the same time. It is a kind of self portrait, but you couldn't recognize Hatoum from these images. *Corps étranger* is French for "foreign body." Some people think this title is meant to refer to Hatoum's own flesh, made "foreign" or unfamiliar by being shown in this way. But for others, the "foreign bodies" are actually those of the viewers themselves, intruding into an intimate, enclosed space where they don't really belong.

Fame and fortune

Works of modern art often sell for vast sums, a fact that puzzles or even angers many people. It can be difficult to justify the high prices. Modern art covers such a broad range of ideas and approaches, it is impossible to get everyone to agree on what things are worth. This spread looks at the awkward question of how art is valued and sold.

👁 For a link to a website where you can see details of the top ten most expensive paintings, go to www.usborne-quicklinks.com

What's it worth?

The price of a work of art depends on the artist's reputation, current fashion and the state of the art market, as well as the cost of making that work. Rare works are more valuable, so prices often rise after an artist's death. Today, most art is sold by dealers or at auctions. Dealers set their own prices, keeping a percentage of the cost to cover their expenses. If art is auctioned, the price is decided by what people are prepared to bid at the sale.

The record for the most expensive painting is held by Pablo Picasso's *Boy with a Pipe*. In May 2004, it fetched $104 million at auction, beating the previous record-holder, Vincent van Gogh's *Portrait of Dr. Gachet*, which raised $82.5 million in 1990. But records like these reflect only what has come up for sale. A lot of art in museums has never been auctioned and is considered priceless.

Art and money

Some artists have fought against the way they see money dominating art. For example, some 1960s artists chose to make Environmental or Performance art, precisely because it couldn't be bought and sold. Ironically, though, it often had to be financed by art market sales of photographs showing the finished work, or drawings of the artists' plans.

In 2001, British artist Michael Landy created a radical performance piece entitled *Break Down*. He wanted to protest about contemporary values and the emphasis society puts on owning and consuming things. So he organized a team of workers to destroy everything he possessed, from his car to a favorite sheepskin coat. After two weeks, he was left with just the clothes he was wearing and his pet cat. The event was paid for by sponsors, who were meant to receive the debris afterward. But Landy decided to bury it instead – perhaps to ensure it could never be sold.

The auction of Picasso's *Boy with a Pipe* at Sotheby's in New York attracted some of the highest ever bids. Picasso painted this picture when he was only 24 and still struggling to make ends meet.

Collector's items

Bunny (1997), by Sarah Lucas; tights, chair, clamp, stuffing and wire, 40 x 35 x 25in. This provocative figure is one of the works in the Saatchi Gallery, London. The half-woman, half-rabbit, headless body mocks the idea of attractive women posing as "playboy bunnies."

In the past, wealthy patrons and collectors had a huge influence on art. Most artists worked for patrons, who commissioned them to make paintings or sculptures to order. But, during the 19th century, more art came to be sold through dealers, who sell uncommissioned art directly to the public. This gave artists more creative freedom – though they still needed to sell their work to earn a living.

Most art continues to be sold through dealers today. But individual collectors can have a big impact, setting fashions and creating new museums. American heiress Peggy Guggenheim founded the Guggenheim Museum in Venice, and advertising millionaire Charles Saatchi set up the Saatchi Gallery in London. Saatchi has also done a lot to promote young British artists, such as Damien Hirst and Sarah Lucas. His critics say that he deliberately selects controversial art in order to make headlines. Once the art is better known, it fetches a higher price, so he can sell it on at a profit. But Saatchi himself claims big museums neglect young artists and says he is trying to fill a gap.

Award winners

Another way for artists to gain recognition is through contemporary art prizes. There are several European awards, but the Turner Prize in Britain is perhaps the best known. This prize has often been the focus of fierce protests, including egg-throwing, graffiti and demonstrators in clown suits. In 1993, two millionaire musicians known as the "K Foundation" decided to award a prize to Britain's worst artist, to be chosen from the real Turner Prize shortlist. Sculptor Rachel Whiteread won both prizes, and gave the K Foundation prize money to charity.

But the Turner Prize is not always so controversial. When potter Grayson Perry won in 2003, there was little argument – despite his unusual dress sense. His delicately crafted vases, with titles such as *Boring Cool People* or *We Are What We Buy*, seemed to unite critics in praise of his artistic skill and handling of difficult subjects.

Here, the potter Grayson Perry (who is a man, but likes to wear women's clothes) poses with one of his award-winning vases at the Turner Prize ceremony.

For links to websites where you can see more works from The Saatchi Gallery, London, or find out all about Britain's Turner Prize, go to **www.usborne-quicklinks.com**

79

Timeline

These two pages list many of the important dates in modern history, and in the history of modern art, so you can see what was happening at particular times.

For links to websites where you can see timelines of the history of art, and find out more about different periods and styles, go to **www.usborne-quicklinks.com**

1825 The first passenger railway opens.

1838 Louis Daguerre invents early photographs, or "daguerreotypes."

1841 John Rand patents the collapsible metal paint tube.

1848 The "Year of Revolution" sees uprisings across Europe; the Communist Manifesto is published.

1853 Baron Haussman starts building the wide Paris streets known as boulevards.

1870-80s Impressionism

1872 Monet paints *Impression: Sunrise;* the title gives rise to the name Impressionism.

1874 The first Impressionist exhibition is held in Paris.

1880s Seurat develops Pointillism; Cézanne experiments with perspective.

1885 German Karl Benz builds the first motor car.

1888 George Eastman mass markets "Kodak" cameras; van Gogh moves to Arles and begins painting sunflowers; Gauguin gives a painting lesson to Sérusier, helping him to create *The Talisman.*

1889 The Eiffel Tower is built in Paris; a decade later it inspires Delaunay to create a series of Cubist paintings.

1890 Van Gogh commits suicide.

1891 Gauguin travels to Tahiti.

1892 Secession of dissenting artists in Munich.

1895 Munch creates *The Scream.*

1897 Secession in Vienna; the Tate Gallery is founded in London.

1899 Secession in Berlin.

1900 Psychoanalyst Sigmund Freud publishes "The Interpretation of Dreams;" his theories later inspire the Surrealists.

1903 The Wright brothers make the first successful powered flight in America.

1905-20s Expressionism

1905 Matisse and Derain spend the summer painting at Collioure, France; they and a group of fellow artists earn the nickname *Fauves; Die Brücke* is formed in Germany.

1906 Cézanne memorial exhibition in Paris; visitors include Picasso and Braque.

1907-20s Cubism

1907 Picasso and Braque begin to develop Cubist techniques; Picasso paints *Les Demoiselles d'Avignon.*

1908 Braque paints *Houses at L'Estaque,* described as resembling "a pile of little cubes," giving rise to the name Cubism.

1909-14 Futurism

1909 The First Futurist Manifesto is issued.

1910 Abstract art begins

1910 The Futurists issue a *Technical Manifesto;* Kandinsky begins experimenting with abstract art.

1911 Kandinsky and Marc found *Der Blaue Reiter* movement in Germany.

1912 Picasso creates *Still Life with Chair Caning,* one of the first collages.

1913 Malevich begins to work on Suprematism; Duchamp attaches a bicycle wheel to a kitchen stool to create *Bicycle Wheel,* the first readymade.

1913-14 Balla paints *Abstract Speed + Sound.*

1914 Wyndham Lewis founds the Vorticist movement in Britain.

1914-18 First World War – millions die during the conflict, which sees introduction of poison gas, planes and machine guns.

1916-24 Dada

1916 Dada movement founded by artists and writers protesting against the war; first performances at the Cabaret Voltaire; Spencer goes to Macedonia with the Royal Army Medical Corps.

1917 Russian Revolution; Society of Independent Artists refuse to exhibit Duchamp's readymade *Fountain;* van Doesburg founds *De Stijl* magazine in Holland.

1919 Bauhaus art and design school founded in Weimar, Germany; Spencer paints *Travoys Arriving with Wounded.*

1920 First Constructivist group forms in Russia; its members create many designs for the new Russian government during the early 1920s.

1921 Third International Communist Congress held in Moscow; but the monument designed by Tatlin to commemorate it never gets beyond a large-scale model.

late 1920s Stalin's government suppresses Constructivism and promotes Soviet Socialist Realism instead.

1924-40s Surrealism

1924 Surrealism is founded in Paris.

1925 First Surrealist exhibition is held

1926 Bauhaus moves to Dessau, Germany.

1926-28 Van Doesburg designs the interior of the Café d'Aubette in Strasbourg and dedicates a whole issue of *De Stijl* to the project.

1929 Start of the Great Depression – many countries undergo economic crisis; the Museum of Modern Art is founded in New York.

1931 Dalí paints *The Persistence of Memory.*

1932 Marinetti publishes a *Futurist Cookbook* aimed at revolutionizing food.

1933 Nazi leader Adolf Hitler comes to power in Germany; the Nazis close Bauhaus; artist and pacifist John Heartfield is forced to leave Germany.

1937 Nazi exhibition of "degenerate" art opens in Munich, then tours to other German cities; after it closes, the art is sold to other countries or burned.

1938 Chagall paints *White Crucifixion;* Dali creates *Lobster Telephone,* probably the most famous Surrealist object.

1939-45 Second World War.

1940s-50s Abstract Expressionism

1942 Hopper paints *Nighthawks.*

1943-44 Hepworth creates *Wave.*

1944 Bacon paints *Three Studies for Figures at the Base of a Crucifixion.*

late 1940s Pollock develops Action painting; Rothko begins to create Color Field paintings.

1950s-60s Minimalism, Conceptual art and Pop art

1950s Acrylic paints invented.

1956 Hamilton makes *Just What Is It That Makes Today's Homes So Different, So Appealing?*

1957 Klein patents an intense blue color called "International Klein Blue."

1959 The Solomon R. Guggenheim Museum opens in New York.

1960s Land art begins

1960 Tinguely's Kinetic sculpture *Homage to New York* self-destructs at the Museum of Modern Art, New York.

1960s First exhibition of Minimalist Art.

1960-61 Klein stages the *Anthropometries* performances.

1961 Russian Yuri Gagarin is first man in space.

1963 Lichtenstein paints *Whaam!*

1964 Warhol creates *Elvis I & II.*

1965 Beuys performs *How to explain paintings to a dead hare;* Kosuth creates *One and Three Chairs.*

1966 Andre creates *Equivalent VIII* out of firebricks; ten years later, there is a huge controversy when it is bought by London's Tate Gallery.

1967 Blake designs the cover for the Beatles' *Sgt. Pepper* album; Hockney paints *A Bigger Splash.*

1969 U.S. astronaut Neil Armstrong walks on the moon.

1970s-80s Sherman produces her series of *Untitled Film Stills.*

1977 De Maria creates *The Lightning Field* in New Mexico; the Pompidou Center opens in Paris, displaying an important collection of modern art.

1979 Peggy Guggenheim donates her home and art collection for a modern art museum in Venice.

1980s Hockney begins to work with photomontage.

1981 Kruger creates *Your Gaze Hits the Side of My Face.*

1983 The Turner Prize is founded in Britain.

1984 Charles Saatchi opens the Saatchi Gallery in London, displaying his controversial collection of modern art.

1985 Protest group the Guerilla Girls form in New York; Basquiat paints *Gas Truck.*

1986 Koons creates *Rabbit.*

1987 Goldsworthy makes *Icicle Star.*

1988 Hirst organizes an exhibition called "Freeze" in a disused warehouse, helping to launch many young British artists.

1989 Long makes *Mud Hand Circles* on a wall in Jesus College, Cambridge.

1990s Britart

1990 Van Gogh's *Portrait of Dr. Gachet* breaks art-market records by selling for U.S. $82.5 million.

1991 Parker makes *Cold Dark Matter;* Quinn sculpts *Self* using his own blood; Hirst creates *The Physical Impossibility of Death in the Mind of Someone Living.*

1993 Whiteread creates *House,* a sculpture cast from the inside of a real house; the "K Foundation" announces an anti-Turner prize to be awarded to Britain's worst artist; both this and the real prize are won by Whiteread.

1994 Hatoum creates *Corps étranger.*

1995 Kapoor creates *Turning the World Inside Out;* Christo and Jeanne-Claude complete their project *Wrapped Reichstag.*

1996 Ofili creates *Afrodizzia.*

1997 The "Sensation" exhibition of young British artists opens in London, causing a storm of controversy; it later transfers to Hamburg and then New York, where the mayor threatens to close it down; a new Guggenheim Museum opens in Bilbao; Mueck creates *Angel;* Antony Gormley's jumbo-jet sized *Angel of the North,* Britain's largest sculpture, is unveiled.

1999 Bourgeois creates *Maman;* Wallinger's *Ecce Homo* is displayed in London's Trafalgar Square; Emin's *My Bed* is nominated for the Turner Prize.

2000 Whiteread's memorial to concentration camp victims is unveiled in Vienna; Tate Modern opens in London.

2001 Viola creates *Five Angels for the Millennium.*

2004 Picasso's *Boy with a Pipe* sells for a record U.S. $104 million at auction; Taylor-Wood's film of soccer player David Beckham sleeping draws huge crowds at the National Portrait Gallery, London; Perry wins the Turner Prize; major artworks by Hirst, Emin and others are destroyed in a fire at a London warehouse.

About the artists

If you want to find out more about the artists in this book, you can read short biographies of them here.

For even more information, go to **www.usborne-quicklinks.com**, where you will find links to some useful websites.

Carl ANDRE (Born 1935)
American sculptor. Associated with Minimalism. Started out working on railways, which gave him the idea of using standard, repeated elements, such as bricks.

Hans ARP (1887-1966)
German-born painter and sculptor. Joined the Dada group in Zurich during the First World War. Later developed his own abstract, geometric style. Worked with **van Doesburg** on the Café d'Aubette.

Francis BACON (1909-1992)
Irish-born British painter. Friend of **Freud**. Worked as an interior designer before turning to painting. Developed a dramatic, Expressionist style. Many of his paintings feature distorted human figures, often based on portraits of friends.

Hugo BALL (1886-1927)
German writer. Founded the Cabaret Voltaire in Zurich in 1916 and took part in Dada performances there.

Giacomo BALLA (1871-1958)
Italian artist. First worked as an illustrator, caricaturist and portrait painter. Founded Futurism with **Marinetti**. He also designed Futurist furniture and clothing.

Jean-Michel BASQUIAT (1960-1988)
Hispanic-African-American painter. Became famous as a graffiti artist in New York, going by the tag "Samo." Later worked with **Warhol**. His exuberant, aggressive style had great commercial success. Died from a drug overdose at the age of only 28.

Joseph BEUYS (1921-86)
German artist. Studied medicine, then joined the air force in 1940. After WWII, dedicated his life to art. Made professor of sculpture at Düsseldorf Academy in 1961. Dismissed for allowing 50 rejected students to

attend his classes. Became increasingly involved in politics. Believed that art could change society, and that "everyone is an artist."

Peter BLAKE (born 1932)
British artist. Associated with Pop art. Uses comics and magazines to make collages, often including cult figures such as Marilyn Monroe. Has also designed record covers.

Fritz BLEYL (1880-1966)
German architect. One of the founders of the Expressionist group, *Die Brücke*, with his friends **Kirchner, Schmidt-Rottluff** and **Heckel**.

Umberto BOCCIONI (1882-1916)
Italian painter and sculptor. Knew **Marinetti** and helped write the Futurists' *Technical Manifesto*. Pioneered Futurist sculpture, sometimes in mixed media. Enlisted in the army in WWI and was killed falling from a horse.

Louise BOURGEOIS (born 1911)
French-American sculptor. Studied in Paris with **Brancusi** and **Giacometti**. Creates sculptures and installations using many different media including metal, wood and fabric. Much of her work explores the body, power and surveillance.

Constantin BRANCUSI (1876-1957)
Romanian-French sculptor. Moved to Paris in 1904, where he became friends with **Matisse** and **Picasso**. Known for his strikingly original, modern-looking works such as *Bird in Space*.

Georges BRAQUE (1882-1963)
French artist. Was a decorator before studying art in Paris. Influenced by the Impressionists and Fauves. Worked closely with **Picasso** developing Cubism from 1907 until 1914, when he was called up.

André BRETON (1896-1966)
French poet and leader of the Surrealists. Argued Surrealism should include art when many of its supporters believed it should be a strictly literary movement.

Paul CEZANNE (1839-1906)
French painter. Abandoned legal studies to become a painter. Worked in Paris where he met **Pissarro**, **Monet** and **Renoir**. Then moved back to southern France and turned his attention to landscapes, developing an almost geometric way of working. Greatly influenced the Cubists.

Marc CHAGALL (1887-1985)
Russian-born painter. Influenced by Expressionism and Cubism, as well as his own Jewish background. Many of his works celebrate Russian-Jewish culture or reflect personal feelings.

CHRISTO (born 1935)
Bulgarian sculptor. Works largely in the U.S. Has become famous, with his wife Jeanne-Claude, for creating large-scale outdoor works by wrapping things, or using fencing or umbrellas.

Chuck CLOSE (born 1940)
American painter. Associated with Photorealism and known for his incredibly lifelike, detailed pictures of family and friends. Had to adapt his methods after he was badly disabled in 1988, and developed a looser, more colorful style.

Salvador DALI (1904-89)
Spanish artist, designer and writer. Expelled from the Madrid Academy of Art. Moved to Paris and met **Picasso** and **Miró**. Became a leading Surrealist, making movies and paintings illustrating the world of the unconscious. Went to the U.S. to avoid WWII. Flamboyant and eccentric, he once gave a lecture in an old-fashioned diving suit, accompanied by two wolfhounds. He claimed, "The only difference between me and a madman is that I am not mad!"

Edgar DEGAS (1834-1917)
French artist. Studied law then art. Known for his paintings of dancers, racehorses and city life. Also made pastels and sculptures exploring movement. Exhibited with the Impressionists, but didn't share all their ideas. Became a recluse in old age.

Robert DELAUNAY (1885-1941)
French painter. Made stage sets, then turned to art. Interested in color theory and Cubism. Known for his almost abstract pictures of colored circles.

Walter DE MARIA (born 1935)
American sculptor. Associated with Land Art. His works include filling a gallery with soil up to waist height, and *Lightning Field*, an installation of 400 steel poles arranged in a grid in a field in New Mexico.

André DERAIN (1880-1954)
French painter. Studied alongside **Matisse**. In his youth, known as one of the Fauves. Later experimented with Cubism, and knew **Picasso** and **Braque**.

Otto DIX (1891-1970)
German painter. Influenced by **van Gogh** and the Futurists. Fought in WWI and afterward war became a dominant theme in his work. Known for his satirical paintings about social corruption. After WWII, turned to religious subjects.

Marcel DUCHAMP (1887-1968)
French artist. Worked as a librarian while studying art. Early paintings were influenced by Cubism. Became a leader of the Dada and Surrealist movements in New York. His "readymades" changed people's views about what constitutes art. Also a professional chess player.

Tracey EMIN (born 1963)
British artist. Associated with Britart. Works include paintings, prints and sculptures, as well as installations. Much of her work is autobiographical.

Dan FLAVIN (born 1933)
American artist. Associated with Minimalism, but said the label was "objectionable." Specializes in sculptures using fluorescent light tubes.

Lucian FREUD (born 1922)
British painter. Grandson of Sigmund Freud and friend of **Bacon**. His subjects are often people in his life, such as friends, relatives and lovers.

Paul GAUGUIN (1848-1903)
French painter and sculptor. A sailor and then a stockbroker, he gave up his job to become an artist, but found it hard to make ends meet. He developed a flat, colorful style which influenced the Nabis. Worked in rural France, at one point living with **van Gogh**, then went to Tahiti, where he died.

Mark GERTLER (1891-1939)
British painter. Son of Polish-Jewish immigrants. Studied in London along with **Spencer**. Painted *Merry-Go-Round*, considered by many critics to be the most important painting of WWI. Depressed by ill health and inability to sell paintings, he committed suicide in 1939.

Alberto GIACOMETTI (1901-66)
Swiss sculptor and painter. Son of a painter. Known for his sculptures of eerily thin figures. Friend of **Picasso** and writers Simone de Beauvoir, Jean-Paul Sartre and Samuel Beckett.

GILBERT and GEORGE
Two artists, Gilbert (Proesch, born in Italy in 1943) and George (Passmore, born in Britain in 1942). Initially known as performance artists, always wearing identical suits. Many early works featured them as "living sculptures." Later works include films, installations and large, colorful photomontages, often using shocking images.

Andy GOLDSWORTHY (born 1956)
British artist. Worked on a farm as a teenager, forming an interest in nature. Makes sculptures from natural materials, often designed to be temporary, such as *Midsummer Snowballs* (2000) – giant snowballs which melted to reveal feathers, leaves and other objects buried inside.

Francisco de GOYA (1746-1828)
Spanish painter. Worked in Madrid, creating elegant portraits and paintings of everyday scenes. Also known for his shocking scenes of war and nightmares.

Juan GRIS (1887-1927)
Spanish painter and sculptor. Real name José Gonzalez. Moved to Paris, met **Picasso** and joined the avant-garde. But progressed slowly until an art dealer gave him a contract. Became a leading Cubist.

Walter GROPIUS (1883-1969)
German architect and teacher. Set up Bauhaus, an art school where all students studied arts, crafts and design.

The GUERILLA GIRLS (founded 1985)
Anonymous group of women artists based in New York. Formed to campaign on issues such as sexism and racism in film, art and politics. Members use the

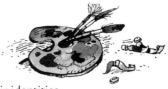

names of dead women artists and wear gorilla masks to hide their identities.

Richard HAMILTON (born 1922)
British artist. His art studies were interrupted by WWII, when he worked as a draftsman. After the war, became a leading Pop artist. Also an influential teacher and writer.

Mona HATOUM (born 1952)
Palestinian-born artist. Has lived in Britain since 1975. Became known in the 1980s for her performance work. Since then, has concentrated on video, installations and sculptures, focusing on themes such as violence and oppression.

John HEARTFIELD (1891-1968)
German artist. Born Helmut Herzfelde but changed his name in 1916 to protest against German nationalism. Best known for his satirical photomontages.

Erich HECKEL (1883-1970)
German painter. Formed the Expressionist group *Die Brücke* with his friends **Kirchner, Schmidt-Rottluff** and **Bleyl**. During WWII the Nazis condemned his art as "degenerate" and much was destroyed.

Barbara HEPWORTH (1903-1975)
British sculptor. Created geometric and organic forms pierced with holes. Was friends with **Moore** and influenced his work.

Damien HIRST (born 1965)
British artist. Achieved notoriety with his provocative works using dead animals suspended in preservative. Has also made works inspired by pharmaceutical products. Once created an arrangement of garbage for a London gallery, only to have a cleaner clear it away by mistake.

David HOCKNEY (born 1937)
British artist. Born in the north of England, but moved to California in the 1960s. Associated with Pop art, though hates the label. Known for his portraits and pictures of swimming pools, painted in a clean, flat style. Has also experimented with photos, faxes and photocopies, and designed stage sets for operas.

Edward HOPPER (1882-1967)
U.S. painter. Also worked as a commercial illustrator. Admired for his realistic, atmospheric landscapes. His use of moody lighting helped create a distinctive American style.

Gary HUME (born 1962)
British painter. Known for his glossy images of everything from doors and flowers to Michael Jackson's face after plastic surgery. Describes himself as "a beauty terrorist."

Jean-Auguste-Dominique INGRES (1780-1867)
French painter. Known for his smooth, polished style. A successful portrait artist.

JEANNE-CLAUDE See **CHRISTO**

Donald JUDD (1928-1994)
U.S. artist. Known as a Minimalist sculptor though he disliked the label. Worked with industrial materials, such as sheet metal and plywood. His later works were built by professional metal workers.

Vassily KANDINSKY (1866-1944)
Russian painter. Studied law before turning to art. Worked in Germany, Russia and France. Founded *Der Blaue Reiter* with **Marc**. One of the first abstract artists.

Taught at the Bauhaus. Had many works confiscated by the Nazis. In 1933, moved to France, where he worked with **Miró**.

Anish KAPOOR (born 1954)
Indian-British sculptor. Grew up in Bombay, but came to London to study art. Creates abstract forms, sometimes covered with bright pigments imported from India. Says he wants his sculptures to look as if they have come 'from another world."

Ernst KIRCHNER (1880-1938)
German artist. Helped found *Die Brücke*. Discharged from the army during WWI because of a mental breakdown. Created several frescoes while recovering. In 1937, the Nazis condemned his art as "degenerate." Committed suicide in 1938.

Yves KLEIN (1928-62)
French artist. Studied judo and languages before turning to art. Worked with

natural substances such as pure pigment, gold leaf and real sponge. Loved intense colors and patented his own shade of blue. Also staged performances and, in 1958, exhibited bare walls in a Paris gallery. Later experimented with fire and water.

Gustav KLIMT (1862-1918)
Austrian artist. Set up a firm in Vienna producing mosaics and murals, and had a great influence on decorative art. A leading artist in the Secession in Vienna. Probably best-known for his painting *The Kiss* (1908).

Jeff KOONS (born 1955)
U.S. artist. Creates sculptures out of inflatable toys and other kitsch objects. Also works with photography.

Joseph KOSUTH (born 1945)
U.S. artist. Trained in New York. Known for his Conceptual artworks using dictionary definitions of words.

Barbara KRUGER (born 1945)
U.S. artist. Started out designing magazines. Her art combines magazine-style photographs and slogan-like text. It is designed to challenge viewers to think about political issues such as feminism and consumer culture.

Michael LANDY (born 1963)
British artist. Creates installations and performances. Probably best-known for his work *Break Down*, where he cataloged and destroyed all his possessions.

Roy LICHTENSTEIN (1923-97)
American painter and sculptor. A university teacher and leading Pop artist. Began painting cartoons after one of his sons pointed to a comic book and challenged him to do better. Known for his striking comic-strip images, painted to mimic cheap printing processes.

Richard LONG (born 1945)
British artist. Known for making Land art based on long walks in remote areas, from the Arctic Circle to the Himalayas. Also uses natural materials such as mud and stones to create indoor works.

Sarah LUCAS (born 1962)
British artist. Associated with Britart. Uses everyday objects, often arranged in a humorous way, to create challenging works about subjects such as sex and death.

René MAGRITTE (1898-1967)
Belgian artist. Briefly earned a living designing wallpaper and drawing fashion advertisements. Knew the Surrealists, including **Dali** and **Miró**, and developed his own version of Surrealism. His paintings only received wide attention after WWII, and have since influenced posters and advertising.

Kasimir MALEVICH (1878-1935)
Russian painter. Experimented with various styles, and invented Suprematism, the abstract geometric style for which he is known. Designed opera costumes and scenery. Also an art teacher and theorist.

Franz MARC (1880-1916)
German painter. Son of a landscape painter. Founded the group *Der Blaue Reiter* with **Kandinsky**. Explored colors in a way partly inspired by **Delaunay**, and developed his own Expressionist style. He often painted animals, and gave lessons in animal anatomy. Killed in WWI.

F.T. MARINETTI (1876-1944)
Italian poet. Creator and leader of the Futurist movement. Author of the first Futurist Manifesto and the *Futurist Cookbook*.

Henri MATISSE (1869-1954)
French painter and sculptor. Abandoned law studies to become an artist. Leader of the Fauve group and known for using bright, decorative colors. Mainly painted women, interiors and still lifes. Influenced the Expressionists but, unlike them, tried to represent happy emotions. With **Picasso**, one of the most influential artists of the 20th century. Admired **Cézanne** and bought Cézanne's small painting *Bathers* in 1899, which he claimed sustained him spiritually through hard times. Said that art should be soothing and restful, like a "good armchair."

MICHELANGELO (1475-1564)
Italian artist. Known to his contemporaries as the "Divine Michelangelo." Hugely influential, his most famous works include the giant statue *David* and the frescoes in the Sistine Chapel in the Vatican.

Joan MIRO (1893-1983)
Spanish painter. Exhibited with the Surrealists in Paris. Became known for his

quirky, detailed paintings, though later simplified his style. Also did sculptures, etchings and murals.

Piet MONDRIAN (1872-1944)
Dutch painter. Began painting traditional landscapes, but soon made them brighter and more stylized. His work became more linear and abstract, until it was a grid of black lines with blocks of primary colors. Leading member of Dutch art and design movement known as *De Stijl*.

Claude MONET (1840-1926)
French painter. Loved painting outside, directly from nature. His chief concern was the changing effect of natural light. Worked

with **Renoir**, **Pissarro** and others to develop Impressionism – the name was taken from criticism leveled at his picture *Impression: Sunrise* (1872). Probably best-known for his water lily paintings, made in his garden at Giverny in northern France. In later life, he suffered from cataracts – an eye condition which makes people see things in muddy, red or yellowish tones. These colors feature strongly in his paintings from 1905 until 1923, when he had an operation to cure it.

Henry MOORE (1898-1986)
British sculptor. Influenced by ancient sculptures and by **Hepworth**, with whom he studied. Early in his career, he carved sculptures from wood and stone, often depicting figures or family groups. During WWII, a lack of available materials led him to turn to drawing. Famously sketched people sheltering from bombs in the London Underground. After the war, he turned mainly to large bronze castings, often of reclining women, or mothers and children.

Ron MUECK (born 1948)
Australian-born artist. Started out making puppets and models for films. Creates extremely detailed figures using specialist techniques developed for films. Some of his sculptures are larger than life, and some smaller; none are actually life-size. Son-in-law of **Rego**.

Edvard MUNCH (1863-1944)
Norwegian painter. Influenced by **van Gogh**, he made intense, emotion-filled paintings and prints. His mother and sister died of TB during his childhood,

and death is a recurring theme in his work. His best-known work, *The Scream* (1893), inspired the Expressionists.

Chris OFILI (born 1968)
British artist. His parents come from Nigeria and much of his work draws on his African roots, as well as cultural references and popular material ranging from contemporary Black music to 1970s comics. Known for his use of elephant dung in his paintings.

Georgia O'KEEFFE (1887-1986)
U.S. painter. Early works included landscapes, townscapes and flowers. Married photographer and art dealer Alfred Stieglitz in 1924. Spent much of her later life in Mexico, painting buildings, landscapes and animal bones. Helped pioneer abstract art in America.

Cornelia PARKER (born 1956)
British artist. Best-known for large-scale installations involving violently destroyed objects, such as silver squashed by a steamroller and objects blown up, or burned by lightning or meteors.

James PEALE (1749-1831)
U.S. painter. Specialized in incredibly lifelike paintings of fruit and flowers and other still lifes. Also painted miniatures and landscapes.

Grayson PERRY (born 1960)
British ceramic artist. Makes pots decorated with challenging images addressing social and political issues. Enjoys attacking stereotypes, including gender, by dressing up as a female character named Claire. Critical of what he sees as the banality of society.

Pablo Ruiz PICASSO (1881-1973)
Spanish painter and sculptor. A child prodigy, encouraged to paint by father, an artist and art teacher. Visited Paris in the early 1900s, then settled there, meeting many writers and artists. Developed Cubism with **Braque**, inspired by African art and **Cézanne**. Continued to experiment all his life, creating many innovative works and becoming one of

the most famous 20th-century artists. As well as paintings, made sculptures and ceramics, and designed stage sets. A very fast worker, he completed an average of 8.7 pictures each day of his adult life.

Camille PISSARRO (1830-1903)
French painter. Knew **Monet**. Earned his living by teaching and painting decorative blinds and fans. A major Impressionist and a great influence on **Cézanne**.

Jackson POLLOCK (1912-56)
U.S. painter. Leading figure of Abstract Expressionism. His early work was influenced by ancient myths, and by the work of **Picasso** and the Surrealists. In the late 1940s, he began his famous "drip" paintings, splashing, dribbling and pouring paint onto canvases laid on the floor. Photos of him at work looked so energetic, the technique was dubbed Action Painting. He also experimented with using sand, glass, cigarette ends and other materials to create texture. He was killed in a road accident at the age of 44.

Lyubov POPOVA (1889-1924)
Russian painter and designer. Pioneered abstract painting with **Malevich**, but later joined the Constructivist movement and gave up painting to work on design projects. Died of scarlet fever.

Marc QUINN (born 1964)
British sculptor. Associated with Britart. Studied at Cambridge University. Many of his works use casts of his own body. Best known for *Self*, a model of his head made from his own blood. Has also worked with frozen flowers.

Robert RAUSCHENBERG (born 1925)
U.S. artist. Studied medicine, then drafted into the U.S. navy in WWII. Studied art after the war. Influenced by Dada and Surrealism, his work combines painting, collage and readymades. Also uses print and photographic processes, and has designed sets and costumes. In 1953, he erased a drawing donated by fellow artist Willem de Kooning to create a work called *Erased de Kooning*.

Paula REGO (born 1935)
Portuguese-born painter and illustrator. Has lived in Britain since 1976. Says illustrated children's books were her greatest influence. Her work explores power, sexuality and social codes. Mother-in-law of **Mueck**.

Pierre-Auguste RENOIR (1841-1919) French painter. Trained as a porcelain painter. Studied with **Monet** and was one of the most successful Impressionists. Painted outdoors, directly from the subject, using soft colors. In later life, he also made sculptures.

Alexander RODCHENKO (1891-1956) Russian artist. Worked with the Constructivists. Also experimented with photography, created theatre designs and made several film documentaries. Early in his career, he worked for **Tatlin**.

Mark ROTHKO (1903-70) Russian-born U.S. painter. A leading Abstract Expressionist. Inspired first by **Miró** and the Surrealists, he later specialized in abstract images. Developed a style known as Color Field painting using huge, blurry blocks of color. In 1970, he committed suicide in his New York studio.

Egon SCHIELE (1890-1918) German artist. Associated with Expressionism. His images of young women were considered so shocking, he was sent to prison in 1912 for obscenity.

Karl SCHMIDT-ROTTLUFF (1884-1976) German artist. Added "Rottluff" to his name because it was where he was born. Helped found *Die Brücke*. His harsh, angular style was condemned by the Nazis, who banned him from painting. After WWII, became a professor in Berlin.

Kurt SCHWITTERS (1887-1948) German artist. Associated with Dada. He developed a style known as "Merz," consisting of 2-D and 3-D collages made out of garbage. Also wrote and performed nonsense poems.

Richard SERRA (born 1939) U.S. sculptor. Worked in steel mills. Now makes huge abstract works using metal.

Paul SERUSIER (1863-1927) French painter. Influenced by **Gauguin**. Founded the Nabis in 1889.

Georges SEURAT (1859-91) French painter and theorist. His ideas on color led him to develop Pointillism, a technique using tiny dots of pure color.

Cindy SHERMAN (born 1954) U.S. artist. Works with photography and film. Does series of pictures, often of herself as a variety of characters in different situations. More recently, she has represented herself in pictures that mimic famous old paintings.

Robert SMITHSON (1938-1973) U.S. artist. Known for his Land art such as *Spiral Jetty*, a huge spiral of mud, rocks and salt crystals in the Great Salt Lake, Utah, U.S.A. Died in an aircrash near Amarillo while working on another piece, *Amarillo Ramp*.

Stanley SPENCER (1891-1959) British painter. Known for his landscapes, portraits and Biblical scenes, painted with expressive and sometimes comic distortion. Served as a medic in WWI and as a war artist in WWII. Known for his scruffy appearance, he was once mistaken for a station porter.

Daniel SPOERRI (born 1930) Romanian-born Swiss artist. Has worked as a poet and author, and in dance, mime and theatre. Self-taught as an artist. Has done Kinetic sculptures and "Happenings," and collaborated with **Tinguely**.

Frank STELLA (born 1936) U.S. artist. Studied at Princeton University. Associated with Minimalism. Creates paintings and prints using bands of color, sometimes in blacks and grays, sometimes in brighter shades.

Vladimir TATLIN (1885-1953) Russian artist and architect. Often referred to as the "father of Constructivism." Worked as a painter and stage designer.

Sam TAYLOR-WOOD (born 1967) British artist. Uses film, video and photography. Works with professional actors, dancers and celebrities, including pop star Kylie Minogue and soccer player David Beckham.

Jean TINGUELY (1925-1991) Swiss sculptor. Best-known for his Kinetic sculptures – busy, electric machines that serve no function.

Theo VAN DOESBURG (1883-1931) Dutch artist. Founded *De Stijl* magazine and, with **Mondrian**, pioneered the style which became known by that name.

Vincent VAN GOGH (1853-90) Dutch painter. An unsuccessful preacher, now one of the most famous artists in the world, though he sold only one painting during his life. He began painting somber rural scenes. Then moved to Paris, met **Degas**, **Gauguin**, **Pissarro** and others, and started doing colorful pictures of flowers, people and local scenery. Later, moved south to set up a studio with Gauguin, but argued violently with him and, suffering from mental illness, cut off part of his own ear. Shot himself two years later.

Bill VIOLA (born 1951) U.S. video and installation artist. Worked at a video studio in Italy and studied Buddhism in Japan, before returning to live in the U.S. Awarded many fellowships for his video work.

Maurice de VLAMINCK (1876-1958) French artist. Started out as a mechanic with hopes of being a professional cyclist. Taught himself to paint. Shared a studio with **Derain** and became one of the Fauves.

Mark WALLINGER (born 1959) British artist. Works include sculptures, photographs and video installations.

Andy WARHOL (1928-1987) U.S. artist. Worked in advertising before getting involved with the U.S. Pop art movement. One of the most famous artists of modern times, known for his repeated prints of images taken from advertising and the media. Also made experimental films, including a six-hour film of a man sleeping, and an eight-hour film of the Empire State Building.

Rachel WHITEREAD (born 1963) British sculptor. Known for making casts of objects ranging from a kitchen sink to a whole house.

Wolf WILLRICH (1867-1950) German painter. Produced Nazi propaganda images and helped organize the "Degenerate Art Exhibition" in 1937. Much of his work was destroyed during and after the war.

Percy WYNDHAM LEWIS (1882-1957) British writer and painter. Influenced by the Futurists, he argued for the value of violence, energy and machines. Was an official war artist in WWII. Stopped painting after he went blind in 1951, but continued writing.

Using the Internet

Throughout this book, we have recommended interesting websites where you can find out more about art. To visit the recommended sites, go to the **Usborne Quicklinks Website** at **www.usborne-quicklinks.com** and type the keywords "modern art." There you will find links to click on to take you to all the sites.

Here are some of the things you can do on the recommended sites:

- Visit virtual art exhibitions with hundreds more examples of modern art.

- Explore interactive timelines.

- Experiment with creating your own works of art.

- View panoramic, 3-D views of an artist's studio.

- Go on an online "art safari," looking at a selection of modern art.

Internet safety

When using the Internet, please make sure you follow these guidelines:

- Children should ask their parent's or guardian's permission before connecting to the Internet.

- When you are on the Internet, never tell anyone your full name, address or telephone number. Children should ask an adult before giving their email address.

- If a website asks you to log in or register by typing your name or email address, children should ask an adult's permission first.

- If you do receive an email from someone you don't know, do not reply to the email.

> ## COMPUTER NOT ESSENTIAL
> If you don't have access to the Internet, don't worry. This book is a complete, self-contained reference book on its own.

Site availability

The links in **Usborne Quicklinks** are regularly reviewed and updated, but occasionally you may get a message that a site is unavailable. This might be temporary, so try again later, or even the next day.

If any of the sites close down, we will, if possible, replace them with suitable alternatives, so you will always find an up-to-date list of sites in **Usborne Quicklinks**.

What you need

Most websites listed in this book can be accessed using a standard home computer and a web browser (the software that lets you look at information from the Internet).

Some sites need extra programs (plug-ins) to play sound or show videos or animations. If you go to a site and do not have the necessary plug-in, a message will come up on the screen. There is usually a button on the site that you can click on to download the plug-in. Alternatively, go to **Usborne Quicklinks** and click on **Net Help**. There, you can find links to download plug-ins.

Internet disclaimer

The websites described in this book are regularly reviewed and the links in **Usborne Quicklinks** are updated. However, the content of a website may change at any time and Usborne Publishing is not responsible for the content of any website other than its own.

We recommend that children are supervised while on the Internet, that they do not use Internet chat rooms, and that parents and guardians use Internet filtering software to block unsuitable material. Please ensure that children read and follow the safety guidelines printed on the left.

For more information, see the **Net Help** area on the **Usborne Quicklinks Website**.

Glossary

Lots of specialist words are used in art. This glossary explains the names and terms used in this book, as well as some other common terms you may come across. Words in **bold** have their own entries.

For a link to websites where you can look up lots more technical terms used in art, go to www.usborne-quicklinks.com

2-D - abbreviation of two-dimensional. Used to describe something which is (or seems to be) flat, such as a drawing of a square.

3-D - short for three-dimensional. Used to describe something which is (or seems to be) solid, such as a cube or a picture of a cube.

abstract art - art that has no recognizable subject matter, but is an arrangement of shapes and colors. Pioneered by Kandinsky.

Abstract Expressionism - an art movement which flourished in New York in the 1940s and 50s. It centered on dramatic abstract paintings. Rothko and Pollock were leading members. See also **Action Painting** and **Color Field Painting**.

acrylic paint - paint made from **pigment** and acrylic resin. Invented in the 1950s and now widely used.

Action Painting - a technique developed by Pollock, which involved dribbling and splashing paint onto a horizontal canvas to try to get an emphatic, expressive effect.

allegory - something which has a hidden symbolic meaning.

Analytical Cubism - an early form of **Cubism** developed by Picasso and Braque in about 1907-12. It involved analyzing real objects and breaking them down into separate elements.

applied art - art that has a practical purpose, such as pottery.

art movement - a group of artists who work together and share ideas, and who often exhibit together, too.

assemblage - **3-D collages**. Pioneered by Picasso and Braque, later taken up by Rauschenberg and others.

automatic drawing - a technique invented by the Surrealists. It involved trying to draw without thinking, as a way of trying to access their unconscious minds.

avant-garde - innovative, cutting-edge art. The term comes from the French name for the advance unit of an army.

Bauhaus - an influential German art school where all students studied art, architecture and design, with the aim of creating a better environment for everyone. It opened in Weimar in 1919, then moved to Dessau and later Berlin. It was closed down by the Nazis in 1933.

Blaue Reiter, Der - an **Expressionist** art **movement** founded in Germany in 1911 by Kandinsky and Marc. The name is German for "The Blue Rider" and came from the title of a journal they published. It broke up in 1914.

Britart - abbreviation of "British art." **Movement** which emerged in Britain in the 1990s. It centered on controversial works by young British artists or **YBAs**.

Brücke, Die - a German **Expressionist** art **movement** founded in 1905 by Kirchner, Heckel, Schmidt-Rottluff and Bleyl. The name means "The Bridge" in German; it was meant to signify a bridge to the future, to a new kind of art. It broke up in 1913, with the approach of WWI.

cartoon - a full-scale drawing on paper, used as a basis for a painting. Nowadays, also used to mean a caricature or funny picture.

collage - a technique where newspaper, wallpaper, fabric and other materials are glued onto the picture surface. Pioneered by Picasso and much used in **Pop art**.

Color Field Painting - a style of abstract painting where pictures are made up from large blocks of color, designed to provoke a strong emotional or spiritual response. Pioneered by Rothko.

color wheel - an arrangement of the three **primary colors** (red, yellow and blue) and the **secondary colors** (orange, green and purple) you get by mixing them. It is shown on page 14.

commission - to pay an artist to produce a work of art to order. Also used to describe a work produced in this way.

complementary colors - colors that lie opposite each other on the **color wheel**. Seen side by side, they contrast very strongly and make each other look brighter.

Conceptual art - art that emphasizes the idea behind a work of art, rather than the work itself. As a **movement**, it flourished in the late 1960s-70s, for example in the work of Kosuth and Long.

Constructivism - an **abstract** art **movement** which grew out of the Russian Revolution of 1917. Its members included Rodchenko and Popova. They wanted to help build a new society by designing clothes, furniture, buildings, etc. using geometric principles. Suppressed by Stalin in the early 1920s.

contemporary art - art of the present day (which is not necessarily the same thing as **modern** art).

Cubism - a style that draws attention to the contradictions involved in making a **2-D** image of a **3-D** scene. It appeared around 1907, in pioneering works by Picasso and Braque. The name came from Braque's painting *Houses at l'Estaque* (1908), which a critic described as looking like "a pile of little cubes." The style is sometimes separated into two versions, **Analytical** and **Synthetic Cubism**.

Dada - an art **movement** formed during WWI. Its members created unconventional, shocking art to protest against the war and the state of society, often staging shows which were an early kind of **Performance art**. "Dada" means "hobby horse" in French, "yes-yes" in Russian or "there-there" in German; it is also a sound made by babies. In fact, the name was meant to be meaningless, picked at random from a dictionary.

decorative art - art, such as embroidery or ornate silverwork, made to decorate other things.

"Degenerate" art - a term used by the Nazis to condemn radical modern art, which they feared was subversive. It included works by Kirchner, Grosz and Picasso. In 1937, the Nazis staged a "Degenerate Art Exhibition" in Munich; this later toured to other German cities. Afterwards, most of the art was sold in other countries; the rest was burned in Berlin in 1939.

drip painting - a technique made famous by Jackson Pollock, where paint is dripped and splashed from a brush, stick or can onto a canvas laid horizontally on the floor.

Earthworks - another name for **Land art**.

engraving - a kind of **print**. First, a picture is "engraved" or cut onto a metal plate. The plate is brushed with ink, so ink fills the hollows. Then a sheet of damp paper is pressed over the plate to pick up the ink.

Environmental art - the name given by French artists Christo and Jeanne-Claude to their kind of outdoor art. They prefer this term to **Land art** because they work in a range of different environments.

etching - a kind of **print** made using a metal plate coated with a protective wax. A picture is "etched" or scratched into the wax, revealing the metal beneath, and acid is used to burn the exposed metal. Then the plate is brushed with ink and printed in the same way as an **engraving**.

Expressionism - an early 20th-century development where artists use exaggerated shapes and colors to try to convey feelings and ideas, rather than showing how things really look. It was inspired by the work of Munch and van Gogh. There were two main groups, **Die Brücke** and **Der Blaue Reiter**. See also **Abstract Expressionism**.

Fauves - the name given to a group of young painters around 1905-10 who used vibrant, unnatural colors. Matisse and Derain were leading members. The name means "wild beasts" in French.

feminism - a political movement which emerged in the 1960s-70s, concerned with ensuring women are valued equally to men.

feminist art - art which supports the ideas behind feminism, for example by using traditionally feminine **media** such as embroidery.

figurative art - also known as **representational art**. Pictures or sculptures which show recognizable people, animals and objects. The opposite of **abstract art**.

fine art - a collective term used to describe painting, sculpture, drawing, print-making and, sometimes, music and poetry. Unlike **applied art** or **decorative art**, fine art has no practical purpose.

Fluxus - a 1960s-70s art **movement** inspired by **Dada**. It focused on spontaneous, unexpected kinds of art, often in the form of **Happenings**. The name was meant to evoke a continuous process of change, or "flux." Beuys was a leading member.

found object - an object which an artist has not made, but has chosen to exhibit as a work of art. It can be a natural object, such as driftwood, or a man-made object, such as a bottle. See also **readymades**.

Futurism - an art **movement** founded in Italy in 1909 by Marinetti. Its members celebrated the energy and speed of machines and city life, and even praised war, stating their goals in aggressive manifestoes. It broke up around the start of WWI.

genre - a particular kind of paintings, such as **portraits, landscapes** and **still lifes**.

gouache - thick, water-soluble paint.

Graffiti art - pictures scrawled on walls in public places, or paintings made in this style.

Happenings - unscripted, bizarre performances, such as Beuys' *How to explain paintings to a dead hare* (see page 64). Developed in the 1960s.

harmonizing colors - colors, such as red and orange, that come next to each other on the **color wheel**. Seen side by side, they seem to blend together.

high culture - traditional art forms, such as paintings, that tend to be expensive and available only to small numbers of people. Often contrasted with **pop culture**.

hyperrealism - also known as super realism. An extremely lifelike style of art, often based on photographs.

iconoclasts - in the past, people who wanted to destroy religious art because they believed it led to idol-worship. Now used to describe anyone who attacks traditional beliefs and ideas.

impasto - a very thick layer of paint. From the Italian word for "paste."

Impressionism - the first major **avant-garde** art **movement**, formed in France in the 1860s. Its members wanted to paint outdoors and study the changing effects of natural light. Their work has a sketchy, spontaneous style. Leading members included Monet, Renoir and Pissarro. The name came from a hostile review of Monet's painting *Impression: Sunrise* (1874). See also **plein air**.

installation - a work of art designed to be set up, or installed, in a particular location. Pioneered by **Dada** and **Surrealist** artists.

Kinetic art - sculptures which move, such as those made by Tinguely.

kitsch - something considered trashy or in bad taste, but sometimes ironically celebrated for that.

Land art - also known as **Earthworks**. An art **movement** which began in the 1960s where artists work within the landscape, using natural materials. Land art is often temporary and made in remote places, so known mainly through photographs and other documents. See also **Environmental art**.

landscape format - a rectangle that is wider than it is tall.

landscapes - paintings where landscape or scenery is the main subject.

lithograph - a kind of **print** made by drawing onto a stone or metal tablet. The tablet is wetted, then coated with ink, which sticks to the lines of the drawing. A print is then taken by laying paper over it.

medieval art - art from the Middle Ages (about 1000-1400).

medium/media - the material used to make an artwork, such as **pastels**, **oil paints** or **collage**. Originally, "medium" meant the liquid, such as oil or acrylic resin, that is mixed with dry **pigment** to make paint. "Media" is the plural of medium.

memento mori - an object such as a skull or a dying flame, used by artists to make you think about death.

Merz - a **collage** technique developed by Schwitters using scraps of everyday garbage. He also made 3-D, room-sized collages known as Merzbau.

Minimalism - an art **movement** developed in the U.S. in the 1960s-70s where the art has little obvious content, so viewers have to examine what is there very closely. Not a formal group, but artists associated with it include Andre and Judd.

mixed media - used to describe art made from more than one material or **medium**.

modern - originally "modern" just meant "of the present." However in art, it can be used to mean a particular period from the mid-19th to early 20th century, when artists made a radical break with the past. More generally, it is used for all art

dating from this period onward. See also **postmodern**.

Modernism - a term used to describe the new artistic and cultural trends that arose during the mid-19th and early 20th century. These were largely about rejecting tradition and experimenting with radical new techniques, in the hope of approaching universal truths. **Impressionism** is one early example; **Abstract Expressionism** is another. See also **Postmodernism**.

movements - groups of artists who share ideas and practices, and often exhibit together, as began happening in the 19th century.

Nabis, the - a group of artists who exhibited together at the end of the 19th century. They were inspired by Gauguin to focus on color. The name is Hebrew for "prophets."

naive art - a term used to describe work by untrained artists.

Neo - Latin for "new." It is sometimes added to the name of earlier art **movements** to describe a more recent revival of their ideas or techniques. For example, Neo-Expressionism was a revival of **Expressionism** in the late 1970s-80s.

New Realism - an art **movement** in 1960s France which explored modern consumer culture, often through works made from discarded items. Sometimes known by its French name, *Nouveau Realisme*.

oil paints - paints made by mixing **pigment** and oil. Often shortened to "oils."

old master - one of many celebrated European painters from about 1500-1800, or a painting by one of them.

Op art - short for "Optical art." An art **movement** in the 1950s-60s where artists used abstract, geometric shapes and patterns to create optical illusions and the impression of movement.

palette - a board on which an artist mixes paint colors. Also used to mean the range of colors used by a particular artist.

pastels - chalky, colored crayons.

patrons - people who pay artists to produce work for them.

Performance art - an art **movement** begun in the 1960s where artists stage live performances. Unlike theatre shows, they do not usually follow a plot. The art exists only as long as the performance, but photographs and documents are sometimes kept. See also **Happenings**.

perspective - a system of rules worked out around 600 years ago and used to create a sense of **3-D** space in a **2-D** drawing. One rule is that objects look smaller as they get farther away. Another rule is that parallel lines, such as train tracks, seem to get closer together and meet at the horizon. There is also "aerial perspective," an effect caused by distance, which makes colors seem to fade and turn blue.

photomontage - the technique of combining sections of different photographs to make a new picture.

photorealism - an incredibly detailed, almost photographic style, such as in paintings by Close.

pieta - Italian for "pity." In art, it usually means a painting or sculpture of the Virgin Mary holding her dead son, Jesus.

pigments - powdered substances used to create paint colors. In the past, they were made by grinding anything from earth to precious stones. In the 19th century, bright chemical pigments were introduced.

plein air - French for "open air." This term is sometimes used to mean the Impressionists' technique of painting outdoors. It is also used to describe the effect they were trying to create.

Pointillism - a technique where painters apply tiny dots of pure, unmixed colors instead of blending colors on a **palette**, to try and achieve a brighter, more vibrant effect. Seen from a distance, the dots seem to blend together. Developed in France in the 1880s-90s by Seurat, who called it "Divisionism."

Pop art - an art **movement** developed in the late 1950s-60s that used images taken from **pop culture**. It celebrated and commented on the boom of pop culture and consumerism which followed the austerity of the war years. Pioneered in London by Hamilton and others; U.S. members included Lichtenstein and Warhol.

pop culture - short for "popular culture." It means television programs, movies, magazines, advertising and other productions aimed at a mass audience. Often contrasted with **high culture**.

portrait format - a rectangle which is taller than it is wide.

portraits - pictures of real people that try to capture a true likeness.

Post-Impressionism - a term used to describe the variety of styles that developed in the 1880s-90s following **Impressionism**. It includes the work of Cézanne, Gauguin and van Gogh.

postmodern - the period following the **modern** era, from the mid to late 20th century.

Postmodernism - a term that emerged in the 1970s to describe the artistic and cultural trends which followed **Modernism**. Postmodernism rejects any distinction between **high** and low **culture**, and the idea that there are universal truths. Instead, it embraces diversity and playfulness. Duchamp's **readymades** and Warhol's use of symbols taken from **pop culture** are two examples.

primary colors - red, yellow and blue. All other colors can be made by mixing these colors together.

prime - to prepare a canvas for painting.

primitive art - art from early or non-industrialized societies.

primitivism - an artistic trend inspired by early history, non-Western cultures and children's art. Includes works of art by Gauguin and Kirchner.

print - any picture made by taking an impression from something else, such as a piece of carved wood or linoleum covered in ink. Often used to make many copies of a picture. Includes **etchings**, **lithographs**, **woodcuts** and **silkscreen prints**.

readymades - a name given by Duchamp to works consisting of ordinary, factory-made objects, which the artist has chosen to present as art.

Realism - often used just to mean "lifelike." More specifically, it is the name of a 19th-century **movement** in art and literature, which focused on ordinary, everyday life.

representational art - see **figurative art**.

Secession - the name adopted by groups of avant-garde artists in Austria and Germany who broke away or "seceded" from traditional art academies.

secondary colors - orange, green and purple. These are the colors you get when you mix two **primary colors** together.

silkscreen print - a kind of **print** made using a silk panel to help distribute ink evenly through a stencil onto paper or fabric. A photographic process can be used to create the stencil. Often used by Warhol.

Soviet Socialist Realism - a realistic but melodramatic style of art, developed for propaganda purposes by the Russian Communist party.

Stijl, De - Dutch for "The Style." An early 20th-century art **movement** aimed at promoting a colorful, **abstract** geometric style in art, architecture and design. Pioneered by van Doesburg and Mondrian.

still life - a painting mainly of motionless objects, such as flowers, food and pots. It can also refer to the actual arrangement of objects. The plural is always written "still lifes" (not "lives"). See also **vanitas**.

Suprematism - an early 20th-century style developed by Malevich, based on abstract geometric shapes. With Dynamic Suprematism, he used more complex compositions to convey a sense of energy and movement.

Surrealism - an art **movement** that developed in Paris in the 1920s-40s, inspired by **Dada** and the writings of psychiatrist Sigmund Freud. The Surrealists, including Dalí, aimed to explore our unconscious minds, often using bizarre, dream-like imagery.

Synthetic Cubism - a kind of **Cubism** developed by Picasso and Braque between about 1912-14. It involved "synthesizing" or building up images from abstract parts, using readymade materials such as newspaper.

tableau-piège - this means "picture-trap." Used to describe a group of objects "trapped" and made into a **3-D** picture. Also a "trap" for the viewer, because what looks like a picture is in fact real objects.

three-dimensional - see **3-D**.

trompe l'oeil - a highly realistic painted device that tries to deceive viewers into thinking they are looking at a real object instead of a painted image. The name means "tricking the eye" in French.

two-dimensional - see **2-D**.

vanitas - a **still life** that is meant to remind viewers of the futility of earthly achievements and encourage spiritual thoughts, by reminding them that success is only temporary and death comes to us all. The name is Latin for "vanity" or "futility."

Vorticism - an **avant-garde** art **movement** based in London. Inspired by **Cubism** and **Futurism**, it tried to promote violent change. It began around 1910, but did not survive the brutal reality of WWI.

woodcut - a **print** made by cutting a picture into a wooden block, leaving raised lines which are coated with ink (unlike an **engraving**, where the ink fills the hollows). The block is then pressed onto paper to make a print.

YBAs - short for Young British Artists. Young artists associated with the recent **Britart** phenomenon. They include Hirst, Lucas and Emin.

Index

Cartoons by Uwe Mayer; sample paintwork by Antonia Miller
Thanks to Rachel Firth, Abigail Wheatley and Minna Lacey for additional research,
and to Alice Pearcey, Rebecca Gilpin and Leonie Pratt for editorial assistance.

First published in 2004 by Usborne Publishing Ltd, 83-85 Saffron Hill, London EC1N 8RT.
First published in the U.S. in 2005
www.usborne.com

Copyright © 2004 Usborne Publishing Ltd.
The name Usborne and the devices ♀ 🌐 are Trade Marks of Usborne Publishing Ltd.

All rights reserved. No part of this publication may be reproduced, stored in a retrieval system
or transmitted in any form or by any means, electronic, mechanical, photocopying,
recording or otherwise, without the prior permission of the publisher.

Printed in Spain

Acknowledgements

Every effort has been made to trace the copyright holders of the material in this book. If any rights have been omitted, the
publishers offer their sincere apologies and will rectify this in any subsequent editions following notification. The publishers are
grateful to the following organizations and individuals for their contributions and permission to reproduce material:

Cover (top row, left to right) detail from *Departing Angel* from *Five Angels for the Millennium* (2001) by Bill Viola, by kind
permission of Bill Viola, photograph by Kira Perov; detail from *The Talisman* (1888) by Paul Sérusier © Archivo Iconografico/
CORBIS; detail from *Dynamic Suprematism* (1915-16) by Kasimir Malevich, Novosti (London); detail from *Stables* (1913) by
Franz Marc © Burstein Collection/CORBIS; **(middle row)** detail from *Street with Prostitutes* (1914-25) by Ernst Kirchner © Scala,
Florence © (for works by E. L. Kirchner) by Ingeborg & Dr. Wolfgang Henze-Ketterer, Wichtrach/Bern; detail from *A Bigger
Splash* (1967) by David Hockney, acrylic on canvas 96 x 96in. © David Hockney; detail from *Sunflowers* (1888) by Vincent van
Gogh © The National Gallery Collection, by kind permission of The Trustees of The National Gallery/ CORBIS; **(bottom row)**
detail from *The Icicle Star, Scaurwater, Dumfriesshire, 12th January 1987* by Andy Goldsworthy © Andy Goldsworthy; detail from

Untitled (Your gaze hits the side of my face) (1981) by Barbara Kruger © Barbara Kruger, COURTESY: MARY BOONE GALLERY, NEW YORK; detail from *Guitar on a Table* (1916) by Juan Gris © Christie's Images/ CORBIS; detail from *Afrodizzia* (1996) by Chris Ofili, COURTESY CHRIS OFILI - AFROCO AND VICTORIA MIRO GALLERY; detail from *Dancing Ostriches from Walt Disney's Fantasia* (1995) by Paula Rego © Paula Rego, courtesy Marlborough Fine Art (London) Ltd.
Page 1 Detail from *A Bigger Splash* (1967) by David Hockney, see credit for pages 58-59. **Pages 2-3** Detail from *Dynamic Suprematism* (1915-16) by Kasimir Malevich, see credit for pages 30-31. **Pages 4-5** Detail from *The Stables* (1913) by Franz Marc, see credit for pages 20-21. **Pages 6-7** *Guitar on a Table* (1916) by Juan Gris © Christie's Images/ CORBIS; *The Physical Impossibility of Death in the Mind of Someone Living* (1991) by Damien Hirst © Damien Hirst; *Vanitas* (1600s) by Unknown Artist, The Art Archive/ Exhibition Asnieres/ Seine 1991/ Dagli Orti (A). **Pages 8-9** *The Snail* (1953) by Henri Matisse, The Art Archive/ Tate Gallery London/ Eileen Tweedy © Succession H. Matisse/ DACS 2004; *Untitled* (1985) by Donald Judd, Stedelijk Museum Amsterdam, art © Judd Foundation, licensed by VAGA, New York/ DACS, London 2004; *Girl with a Kitten* (1947) by Lucian Freud © Lucian Freud, British Council, London, U.K./ Bridgeman Art Library; *Maman* (1999) by Louise Bourgeois © Louise Bourgeois/ © FMGB Guggenheim Bilbao Museoa, 2004, photograph by Erika Barahona-Ede, all rights reserved, total or partial reproduction is prohibited. **Pages 10-11** Detail from *Street with Prostitutes* (1914-25) by Ernst Kirchner, see credit for pages 20-21. **Pages 12-13** *The Swing* (1876) by Pierre-Auguste Renoir © Edémedia/ CORBIS; *Impression: Sunrise* (1872) by Claude Monet © Archivo Iconografico/ CORBIS; *The Boulevard Montmartre at Night* (1897) by Camille Pissarro © The National Gallery Collection, by kind permission of The Trustees of The National Gallery/ CORBIS; *Women on the Terrace of a Café* (1877) by Edgar Degas © Archivo Iconografico/ CORBIS. **Pages 14-15** *A Sunday on La Grande Jatte* (1884-86) by Georges Seurat © Bettmann/ CORBIS; *Sunflowers* (1888) by Vincent van Gogh © The National Gallery Collection, by kind permission of The Trustees of The National Gallery/ CORBIS; *She is Called Vairaumati* (1892) by Paul Gauguin © Alexander Burkatowski/ CORBIS. **Pages 16-17** *The Starry Night* (1889) by Vincent van Gogh, digital image © 2004, The Museum of Modern Art, New York (acquired through the Lillie P. Bliss Bequest, 472.19)/ Scala, Florence; *Self Portrait* (1889) by Vincent van Gogh © Archivo Iconografico/ CORBIS. **Pages 18-19** *The Talisman* (1888) by Paul Sérusier © Archivo Iconografico/ CORBIS; *Henri Matisse* (1905) by André Derain © Explorer, Paris/ Powerstock © ADAGP, Paris and DACS, London 2004; *Open Window, Collioure* (1905) by Henri Matisse © Powerstock © Succession H. Matisse/ DACS 2004. **Pages 20-21** *The Scream* (1895) by Edvard Munch, photograph by J. Lathion © Nasjonalgalleriet Oslo © Munch Museum/ Munch-Ellingsen Group, BONO, Oslo, DACS, London 2004; *Reclining Woman with Green Stockings* (1917) by Egon Schiele © Burstein Collection/ CORBIS; *Street with Prostitutes* (1914-25) by Ernst Kirchner © Scala, Florence © (for works by E. L. Kirchner) by Ingeborg & Dr. Wolfgang Henze-Ketterer, Wichtrach/ Bern; *Stables* (1913) by Franz Marc © Burstein Collection/ CORBIS. **Pages 22-23** *Still Life with Basket* (1888-90) by Paul Cézanne © Archivo Iconografico/ CORBIS; *Fruit* (1820) by James Peale © The Corcoran Gallery of Art/ CORBIS; *Clarinet and Bottle of Rum on a Mantelpiece* (1911) by Georges Braque © Tate, London 2004 © ADAGP, Paris and DACS, London 2004; *Still Life with Chair Caning* (1912) by Pablo Picasso © Scala, Florence © Succession Picasso/ DACS 2004. **Pages 24-25** *Les Demoiselles d'Avignon* (1907) by Pablo Picasso, digital image © 2004, The Museum of Modern Art, New York (acquired through the Lillie P. Bliss Bequest, 333.1939)/ Scala, Florence © Succession Picasso/ DACS 2004; photograph of African masks, Werner Forman Archive/ private collection, New York; photograph of Picasso at work © Bettmann/ CORBIS. **Pages 26-27** *Champs de mars, la tour rouge (The Red Tower)* (1911-12) by Robert Delaunay © L & M SERVICES B. V. Amsterdam 20040207; *The Crowd* (1914-15) by Percy Wyndham Lewis © Tate, London 2004 © Wyndham Lewis and the Estate of Mrs. G. A. Wyndham Lewis by kind permission of The Wyndham Lewis Memorial Trust (a registered charity); *Radiator Building – Night, New York* (1927) by Georgia O'Keeffe, FISK UNIVERSITY GALLERIES, NASHVILLE, TENNESSEE © ARS, NY and DACS, London 2004; photograph of New York skyline © Bettmann/ CORBIS. **Pages 28-29** *Unique Forms of Continuity in Space* (1913) by Umberto Boccioni © Scala, Florence; *Abstract Speed + Sound* (1913-14) by Giacomo Ballà, photograph by Myles Aronowitz © The Solomon R. Guggenheim Foundation, New York, Peggy Guggenheim Collection, Venice 1976 (FN 76.2553 PG 31) © DACS 2004; *Bird in Space* (1923) by Constantin Brancusi © Philadelphia Museum of Art/ CORBIS © ADAGP, Paris and DACS, London 2004. **Pages 30-31** *Improvisation No. 26 (Rowing)* (1912) by Vassily Kandinsky, Stadtische Galerie im Lenbachhaus, Munich, Germany/ Bridgeman Art Library © ADAGP, Paris and DACS, London 2004; *Untitled* (1910) by Lyubov Popova © Christie's Images/ CORBIS; *Dynamic Suprematism* (1915-16) by Kasimir Malevich, Novosti (London). **Pages 32-33** Detail from *Travoys Arriving with Wounded at a Dressing Station at Smol, Macedonia 1916* (1919) by Stanley Spencer, see credit for pages 36-37. **Pages 34-35** *Merry-Go-Round* (1916) by Mark Gertler © Tate, London 2004, by kind permission of Luke Gertler; *Disasters of War: The Same* (1812-13) by Francisco de Goya © Archivo Iconografico/ CORBIS; *The War: Assault under Gas* (1924) by Otto Dix, photograph: akg-images © DACS 2004. **Pages 36-37** *Travoys Arriving with Wounded at a Dressing Station at Smol, Macedonia 1916* (1919) by Stanley Spencer, The Imperial War Museum, London. **Pages 38-39** *Fountain* (1964, replica of 1917 original) by Marcel Duchamp © Burstein Collection/ CORBIS © Succession Marcel Duchamp/ ADAGP, Paris and DACS, London 2004; *Merz picture 32A – Cherry Picture* (1921) by Kurt Schwitters, digital image © 2004, The Museum of Modern Art, New York (Mr. and Mrs. A. Atwater Kent, Jr. Fund, 271954)/ Scala, Florence © DACS 2004; *Who knows where upstairs and downstairs are?* (1964) by Daniel Spoerri, Hamburg Kunsthalle, Hamburg, Germany/ Bridgeman Art Library © DACS 2004. **Pages 40-41** *The Future of Statues* (1937) by René Magritte, Christie's Images, London, U.K./ Bridgeman Art Library © ADAGP, Paris and DACS, London 2004; *The Persistence of Memory* (1931) by Salvador Dalí, digital image © 2004, The Museum of Modern Art, New York (given anonymously, 162.1934)/ Scala, Florence © Salvador Dalí, Gala-Salvador Dalí Foundation, DACS, London 2004. **Pages 42-43** *Oval Hanging Construction Number 12* (1920) by Alexander Rodchenko, digital image © 2004, The Museum of Modern Art, New York

(acquisition made possible through the efforts of George and Zinaida Costakis, and through the Nate B. and Frances Spingold, Matthew H. and Erna Futter, and Enid A. Haupt Funds, 1986)/ Scala, Florence © DACS 2004; *Color Scheme for the Café d'Aubette, Strasbourg – color scheme (preceding final version) for floor and long walls of ballroom* (1927) by Theo van Doesburg, digital image © 2004, The Museum of Modern Art, New York (gift of Lily Auchincloss, Celeste Bartos and Marshall Cogan, 391.1982)/ Scala, Florence; photograph of the Bauhaus Dessau building, Dennis Gilbert/ arcaid.co.uk. **Pages 44-45** *Family Portrait* (c.1939) by Wolf Wilrich, Mary Evans Picture Library/ Weimar Archive; *Adolf, the Superman: Swallows Gold and Spouts Junk* (1932) by John Heartfield, photograph: akg-images © The Heartfield Community of Heirs/ VG Bild-Kunst, Bonn and DACS, London 2004; *White Crucifixion* (1938) by Marc Chagall, Art Institute of Chicago, IL, SA/ Bridgeman Art Library © ADAGP, Paris and DACS, London 2004. **Pages 46-47** *Man Pointing* (1947) by Alberto Giacometti, digital image © 2004, The Museum of Modern Art, New York (gift of Mrs. John D. Rockefeller 3rd, 678.1954)/ Scala, Florence © ADAGP, Paris and DACS, London 2004; *Three Studies for Figures at the Base of a Crucifixion* (c.1944) by Francis Bacon © Tate, London 2004; *Nameless Library* (2000) by Rachel Whiteread, courtesy Rachel Whiteread and Gagosian Gallery. **Pages 48-49** Detail from *Mother and Child: Block Seat* (1983-84) by Henry Moore, photograph by Michel Muller, reproduced by permission of The Henry Moore Foundation. **Pages 50-51** *Number 1* (1948) by Jackson Pollock, digital image © 2004, The Museum of Modern Art, New York (purchase, 77.1950)/ Scala, Florence © ARS, NY and DACS, London 2004; *Number 8* (1952) by Mark Rothko © Christie's Images/ CORBIS © 1998 Kate Rothko Prizel & Christopher Rothko/ DACS 2004; *Ursula's One and Two Picture 1/3* (1964) by Dan Flavin, The Solomon R. Guggenheim Museum, New York, Panza Collection, gift 1992, on permanent loan to Fondo per l'Ambiente Italiano, photograph by Rafael Lobato © SRGF, NY (FN 92.4115 DF 6) © ARS, NY and DACS, London 2004. **Pages 52-53** *Mother and Child: Block Seat* (1983-84) by Henry Moore, photograph by Hui-Wan, reproduced by permission of The Henry Moore Foundation; *Wave* (1943-44) by Barbara Hepworth, Scottish National Gallery of Modern Art/ © Bowness, Hepworth Estate; *Turning the World Inside Out* (1995) by Anish Kapoor © Anish Kapoor, photograph by John Riddy, London, courtesy Lisson Gallery, London. **Pages 54-55** *Nighthawks* (1942) by Edward Hopper © Francis G. Mayer/ CORBIS; *Homage to New York* (1960) by Jean Tinguely, digital image © 2004, The Museum of Modern Art, New York (gift of the artist, 227.1968)/ Scala, Florence © ADAGP, Paris and DACS, London 2004; *Gas Truck* (1985) by Jean-Michel Basquiat, private collection, James Goodman Gallery, New York/ Bridgeman Art Library © ADAGP, Paris and DACS, London 2004. **Pages 56-57** *Whaam!* (1963) by Roy Lichtenstein, The Art Archive/ Tate Gallery, London/ Eileen Tweedy © The Estate of Roy Lichtenstein/ DACS 2004; *Just What Is It That Makes Today's Home So Different, So Appealing?* (1956) by Richard Hamilton, photograph: akg-images © Richard Hamilton 2004, all rights reserved, DACS; *Rabbit* (1986) by Jeff Koons © Jeff Koons. **Pages 58-59** *A Bigger Splash* (1967) by David Hockney, acrylic on canvas, 96 x 96in. © David Hockney. **Pages 60-61** *Elvis I & II* (1964) by Andy Warhol © Art Resource/ Scala © The Andy Warhol Foundation for the Visual Arts, Inc./ ARS, NY and DACS, London 2004; *Sgt. Pepper's Lonely Hearts Club Band* (1967) by Peter Blake © Apple Corps Ltd/ Peter Blake 2004 All Rights Reserved, DACS; *Afrodizzia* (1996) by Chris Ofili, COURTESY CHRIS OFILI - AFROCO AND VICTORIA MIRO GALLERY. **Pages 62-63** Detail from *Departing Angel* from *Five Angels for the Millennium* (2001) by Bill Viola, see credit for pages 70-71. **Pages 64-65** *One and Three Chairs* (1965) by Joseph Kosuth © Joseph Kosuth, Sean Kelly Gallery, New York/ The Museum of Modern Art, New York (Larry Aldrich Foundation Fund, 393.1970 a-c); *¼ Mile or 2 Furlong Piece* (1981-present) by Robert Rauschenberg, photograph by Nicholas Whitman www.nwphoto.com © Robert Rauschenberg/ VAGA, New York/ DACS, London 2004; *Cell (Hands and Mirror)* (1995) by Louise Bourgeois © Louise Bourgeois, Collection Barbara Lee, courtesy Cheim & Read, New York, photograph by Peter Bellamy. **Pages 66-67** *Cold Dark Matter: An Exploded View* (1991) by Cornelia Parker, courtesy the artist and Frith Street Gallery, London © Tate, London 2004; *Breathless* (2001) by Cornelia Parker, courtesy the artist and Frith Street Gallery, London. **Pages 68-69** *Mud Hand Circles* (1989) by Richard Long, courtesy of the artist, photograph by kind permission of the Master and Fellows, Jesus College, Cambridge; *The Icicle Star, Scaurwater, Dumfriesshire, 12th January 1987* by Andy Goldsworthy © Andy Goldsworthy; *Wrapped Reichstag, Berlin* (1971-95) by Christo and Jeanne-Claude © Christo, photograph by Wolfgang Volz. **Pages 70-71** *Pieta* (2001) by Sam Taylor-Wood © the artist, courtesy Jay Jopling/ White Cube (London); *Angel* (1997) by Ron Mueck © Ron Mueck, courtesy Anthony d'Offay Ltd; *Ecce Homo* (1999) by Mark Wallinger © the artist, courtesy Anthony Reynolds Gallery; *Departing Angel* from *Five Angels for the Millennium* (2001) by Bill Viola, by kind permission of Bill Viola, photograph by Kira Perov. **Pages 72-73** *Dancing Ostriches from Walt Disney's Fantasia* (1995) by Paula Rego © Paula Rego, courtesy Marlborough Fine Art (London) Ltd; *Untitled (Your Gaze Hits the Side of My Face)* (1981) by Barbara Kruger © Barbara Kruger, COURTESY: MARY BOONE GALLERY, NEW YORK; *Odalisque* (1814) by Jean-Auguste-Dominique Ingres, The Art Archive/ Musée du Louvre, Paris/ Dagli Orti; *Do women have to be naked to get into the Met. Museum?* (1989) by the Guerilla Girls, courtesy www.guerrillagirls.com. **Pages 74-75** *Untitled Film Still #48* (1979) by Cindy Sherman, courtesy the artist and Metro Pictures; *Happy* (1980) by Gilbert and George © the artists © Tate, London 2004; *My Mother, Los Angeles, Dec. 1982* (1982) by David Hockney © David Hockney, photographic collage, edition 20. **Pages 76-77** *Self* (1991) by Marc Quinn © the artist, courtesy Jay Jopling/ White Cube (London); *Self Portrait* (1997) by Chuck Close, photograph by Ellen Page Wilson, courtesy Pace Wildenstein, New York © Chuck Close, The Museum of Modern Art, New York (gift of Agnes Gund, Jo Carole and Ronald S. Lauder, Donald L. Bryant, Jr., Leon Black, Michael and Judy Ovitz, Anna Marie and Robert F. Shapiro, Leila and Melville Straus, Doris and Donald Fisher, and purchase); *Corps étranger* (1994) by Mona Hatoum © Mona Hatoum, collection Centre Pompidou, Paris, photograph by Philippe Migeat. **Pages 78-79** photograph of the auction in 2004 of the Pablo Picasso work *Boy with a Pipe* (1905) © CHIP EAST/ Reuters/ CORBIS © Succession Picasso/ DACS 2004; *Bunny* (1997) by Sarah Lucas © Sarah Lucas, courtesy Saatchi Gallery, London; photograph of Grayson Perry at the Turner Prize award ceremony (2003), wireimage.com.